# WOMEN
# TEACHING FOR CHANGE

## CRITICAL STUDIES IN EDUCATION SERIES
EDITED BY PAULO FREIRE & HENRY A. GIROUX

# WOMEN TEACHING FOR CHANGE

## Gender, Class & Power

Kathleen Weiler

*Introduction by*
*Henry A. Giroux & Paulo Freire*

CRITICAL STUDIES IN EDUCATION SERIES

**BERGIN & GARVEY PUBLISHERS**
NEW YORK • WESTPORT, CONNECTICUT • LONDON

**Library of Congress Cataloging-in-Publication Data**

Weiler, Kathleen.
  Women teaching for change.

  (Critical studies in education series)
  Bibliography: p. 155
  Includes index.
  1. Women teachers—United States.  2. Feminism—United States.
  3. Education, Secondary—United States.  4. Discrimination in education—United States.
  5. Feminist criticism—United States. I.Title. II. Series.
LB2837.W45  1988       371.1′0088042       87-14604
ISBN 0-89789-127-9 (alk. paper)
ISBN 0-89789-128-7 (pbk. : alk. paper)

Library of Congress Catalog Card Number: 87-14604
ISBN: 0-89789-128-7

First published in 1988

Bergin & Garvey Publishers, One Madison Avenue, New York, NY 10010
A division of Greenwood Press, Inc.

Printed in the United States of America

10 9

# Acknowledgments

*As an undergraduate studying history I was taught to read texts as the product of wider intellectual movements reflecting the concerns and tensions of a particular time and place. And now when I read I try to locate the author as a person of a particular gender, race, and class. But it is only looking back over this work that I see how an individual work is the product of collective concerns. In this case, both my own personal concerns and experiences and the collective ideas of people working within an intellectual and political movement have shaped this work. My experiences as a woman and as a teacher have clearly led me to this topic. At the same time, the arguments and ideas discussed here are the product of collective work, even though they are written by an individual. This work reflects ideas that have been generated by an ongoing debate about the nature of schooling and the limits of teaching in schools. They reflect discussions, reading, and collective work with a number of people concerned with teaching and learning. I benefitted greatly from conversations, seminars, and lecture series at Boston University with Henry Giroux and a number of his other graduate students. I also learned a great deal working with authors when I was an editor of* The Journal of Education *and at present as a member of the editorial collective of* Radical Teacher. *I have learned a great deal from discussions with members of the* Radical Teacher *collective. I have benefitted immeasurably from long and stimulating conversations with Sara Freedman about the meaning of teaching for women and the relationship of families and schools. And I want to thank Henry Giroux, Steve Ellenwood, Maureen Giovannini, Michele Sola, Sara Freedman, and Ann Withorn for their helpful reading of all or parts of this work in manuscript. Paul Breines provided invaluable technical help with the manuscript.*

*If the analysis of schooling and teaching I have presented is the product of a wider theoretical debate, the political and critical pedagogy I have documented here is the collective product of the women I interviewed. These teachers and administrators are in the process of creating a critical pedagogy in their classroom teaching and in their encouragment and support of progressive schooling. Their work should be an inspiration to other teachers. I feel greatly indebted to them for expanding my own thinking about teaching and the limits and meaning of ethnographic research in schools.*

*Last I want to thank my two feminist daughters, Sarah and Emma, for their support and encouragment in what my daughter, Sarah, called "smashing patriarchal hegemony." And most of all I want to thank my husband Peter, who was my best and most careful critic and whose love and support in all respects made this book possible.*

# Table of Contents

# Introduction

*by Henry A. Giroux and Paulo Freire*

Kathleen Weiler has taken on in this book an immense theoretical and political project, a project born out of her recognition of the strengths and weaknesses of different strands of radical educational theory as they have developed within the last fifteen years.

Writing as a feminist, Weiler develops a critical theory of schooling that illuminates how gender is socially constructed within institutional and ideological technologies of power that inform all aspects of school life. But Weiler does not limit her analysis to the many disciplinary turns taken by critical pedagogy or feminist theory of schooling over the last few years. On the contrary, she attempts to bridge the most critical aspects of reproduction theory, its emphasis on how wider social forms reproduce the class-specific dimensions of inequality, with those aspects of feminist theory that stress the importance of consciousness, experience, and the subjective side of human relations. While rejecting the class-reductionist and one-sided nature of domination that characterizes both old and new versions of reproduction theories of schooling, Weiler situates her analysis in the view that power, as both the medium and the expression of wider structural relations and social forms, positions subjects within ideological matrixes of constraint and possibility.

The perspective from which Weiler reads the social reality of schooling accents the importance of structural and institutional forces in shaping the ideological and material conditions of the work performed by school administrators and teachers. Yet Weiler is not content to work solely within the language of domination, she also wants to stress the ways in which dominant social forms are contested, resisted, and overcome. In moving beyond the Orwellian despair that characterizes much of radical pedagogy, Weiler rejects the notion that reproduction and resistance are dichotomous social practices; she argues instead that they are mutually informing relations of contradiction that produce forms of social and moral governance, on the one hand, and the regulation of subjects, texts, and subjectivities on the other. This is an important conceptual advance, illuminating how the experiences of both teachers and students, along with the production of knowledge, meaning, and values in schools, can best be understood—by recognizing and analyzing how specific pedagogical practices function within institutional sites to produce contradictory social forms and relations. Within this perspective, Weiler analyzes schools as places that contribute to the production of particular kinds of political identities and subjectivities. Moreover, the experiences that constitute these identities are always contradictory and represent an ongoing struggle between social forms that limit and enable individual capacities. As Philip Corrigan points out:

> At the heart of any analysis of social relations ... there are always contradictions and, consequently, struggles. Generic struggles concern nothing less than the realization of human capacities—being more alive, more happy, less threatened, insecure, and so on—and the blocks that operate on those realizations.[1]

By rejecting the polarities of absolute resistance and absolute domination in various strands of radical educational theory, Weiler attempts to develop a view of consciousness and subjectivity similar to what Sheila Rowbotham calls a "problematic potentiality." Rowbotham writes:

> Problematic potentiality ... [is] never guaranteed yet ... [is] nevertheless possible. Here is the clue to the ambivalence of "needs" which always combine both a reference to the full potential of human nature and, on the other hand, a partial acceptance of the existing order which denies their realization.[2]

In attempting to develop this position further theoretically, Weiler turns to feminist theory to illuminate how human agency is operationalized in particular forms of resistance and struggle. Around and within those particular social forms, relations of power, and institutional configurations of schooling the women in her book fight to reclaim the moral and politically regulated terrains of history, space, time, textuality, desire, and subjectivity. For Weiler, the broader social categories of structure and agency have to be seen as dialectical aspects of the interrelated notions of both reproduction and resistance which, in theoretical and political terms, point to a view of schooling that is much more complex and contradictory than existing ethnographies would suggest.

But the strength of Weiler's book goes far beyond her ability to reconstruct and advance the theoretical gains made by previous radical and feminist theories of education and pedagogy. Weiler also brings into focus a wide range of questions concerning the relations of power and struggles that feminist administrators and teachers have to face in an urban public high school. In doing so, she breaks new theoretical ground, linking the subjective and contextual side of feminist struggle to wider aspects of social and institutional control. What results is an illuminating analysis of how, in Foucault's term, the "technology of power" shapes institutional structures within schools in order to affect the relationships feminist administrators and teachers have with each other, with other members of the administration and faculty, and with students. Ideology in Weiler's view is not only embedded in the discourses, social relations, and experiences that both teachers and students embody and express in schools, it is also deeply ingrained in those institutional practices that shape how time, space, language, and rules constitute and legitimate schooling as a wider field of systematic power and control.[3]

For Weiler, the school is a matrix of institutional, personal, and social forces caught up in deeply contradictory tensions that are neither exclusively dominating nor liberating. Instead, the interests of domination and resistance mutually inform each other, and it is in such contradictory relations that the ideological and material space emerges within schools for developing the insights and forms of radical pedagogy necessary to organize gender, race, and class considerations as part of an emancipatory project.

For those interested in a critical presentation and engagement of critical educational theory and feminist analysis of gender and schooling, Weiler's book provides a succinct and compelling integration. Moreover, Weiler goes beyond the current methodological preoccupation with descriptive accounts and the fetishization of typological distinctions in so many of the ethnographies now being written about education.[4] She provides a critical ethnographic account that is rooted in an emancipatory political project and constructed around a rigorous critical/feminist theoretical discourse. Theory in this case is not merely representational—it plays a constitutive role, articulating the categories, inquiries, and conclusions that give meaning to the experiences and subjective accounts of the feminist administrators and teachers in her study. Weiler narrates how these women struggle, fight, collide with, and support each other. Yet hers is not a narrative presented under the pretense of objective analysis; it is a narrative produced through ideological considerations and interests that confront the realities of school life through a project of possibility, that is, through a project that attempts to study reality in order to change it, to interrogate schooling as an arena of conflict and contestation. She writes in order to promote counterhegemonic strategies which might prove useful to those men and women who are struggling to improve the quality and purpose of schooling in the interests of creating a more just, radically democratic society.

*Women Teaching for Change* challenges the reader to understand schooling and critical pedagogy as a form of cultural politics. By utilizing the concept of "voice" as a pedagogical category to examine the interaction of teachers and learners and the knowledge they both bring to the classroom, as well as the knowledge they produce together, Weiler extends the notion of radical praxis far beyond the ways in which it has been employed in radical educational theory. She rightly criticizes those dogmatic strands within critical pedagogy which assume that a theoretically correct position is all that is needed for students to acquire an alternative reading of the world. She also rejects the prevailing notion that pedagogy necessarily follows from the production or transmission of knowledge. Rather, she takes the position that pedagogy is an integral aspect of knowledge production itself. Finally, Weiler lucidly demonstrates in her study how pedagogy is always part of the dynamic of production, with the teacher rendered as theorist/learner and the student as learner/reader/critic. With a similar clarity of insight, she analyzes how pedagogy, as part of the process of exchange that takes place within asymmetrical relations of power, always engages specific cultural forms and experiences which generate different sets of understandings for teachers and students with respect to the categories of gender, race, and class. In many respects, Weiler's theory of critical pedagogy is about the relations that teachers and students enter into as part of the process of production and exchange around specific forms of knowledge and values and the cultural practices such relations support with respect to dominant or emancipatory interests. The importance of this view of pedagogy is clearly stated by David Lusted and is worth noting. He writes:

> What pedagogy addresses is the process of production and exchange in the cycle, the transformation of consciousness that takes place in the interaction of three agencies: the teacher, the learner, and the knowledge they together produce. ... The concept of pedagogy ... refuses any tendency to instrumentalize the relations, to disconnect their interaction, or to give value to one agency over another. Hence, for instance, it denies notions of the teacher as functionary (neutral transmitter of knowledge as well as "state functionary"), the learner as "empty vessel" or passive respondent,

knowledge as immutable material to impart. Instead, it foregrounds exchange between and over the categories, it recognizes the productivity of the relations, and it renders the parties within them as active, changing, and changeable agencies.[5]

For Weiler, voice is related to the means whereby teachers and students attempt to make themselves *present* in history and to define themselves as active authors of their own worlds. Voice in this sense represents those multiple subjectivities, discourses, and biographies that constitute teachers and students alike within relations of power, history, and experience. As a referent for empowerment, the category of voice interrogates the processes through which identities are ignored, constructed, or experienced; meanings are affirmed, marginalized, or questioned; and experiences are formed within the interlocking and related processes of subjugation, affirmation, and enlightenment.

In *Women Teaching for Change*, Weiler analyzes the contradictions that arise when feminist teachers ignore the voices of their students; points to the subtle ways in which language is used to regulate, silence, and structure expression and expressivity; and shows why such language needs to be reconstructed within a pedagogy that links the production of knowledge and the act of learning to forms of production rooted in the histories, experiences, and meanings of teachers and students. Weiler also utilizes the concept of voice to analyze the interests taken up in teacher discourse and examines how these interests either enable or constrain the possibility for students to affirm their own experiences, challenge the authoritative text of the teacher, and take risks even if the political interests that inform their arguments are at odds with the teacher's discourse. Weiler is aware, too, that the word always belongs to someone else. It becomes "one's own" only, as Mikhail Bakhtin tells us,

> when the speaker populates it with his own intention, his own accent, when he appropriates the word, adapting it to his own semantic and expressive intention. Prior to this moment of appropriation, the word does not exist in a neutral and impersonal language (it is not, after all, out of a dictionary that a speaker gets his words!), but rather it exists in other people's mouths, in other people's contexts, serving other people's intentions: it is from there that one must take the word, and make it one's own.[6]

Weiler's pedagogy is one that celebrates a politics of difference. She is sensitive to the importance of legitimizing the voice of "the other(s)" while simultaneously holding such voices up to interrogation and critique. She seeks to wed intellect and emotional investment around a cultural politics that articulates voice and difference as part of a public philosophy that advances the moral and political imperatives of a radical democracy. In other words, she attempts to develop a critical pedagogy that authenticates voices which challenge prevailing sedimented meanings, celebrate cultural and political diversity, fight against the voices of bigotry and violence, and at the same time work toward social relations that undermine the ideological, experienced relations of sexism, racism, and class discrimination. In addition, she works to develop a critical pedagogy in which radical imperatives are constructed within school and classroom relations, imperatives which take empowerment to mean developing democratic social forms that enlarge and enhance those individual capacities which lend themselves to individual autonomy and collective responsibility and freedom. For Weiler, the language of critique and possibility are dialectically related to both what we teach and how we teach—inseparable activities that bring students and teachers together through the constituting power of both theory and practice, the discourse of radical authority, and the importance of the transformative integrity and force of concrete, lived experience.

*Women Teaching for Change* represents a breakthrough in critical feminist work in its analysis of the achievements and obstacles experienced by feminist administrators and teachers in an urban secondary school. It is a work that reconstructs older traditions in both radical and feminist theories of schooling and pedagogy. But most importantly, it is a book that breaks new ground in linking theory to practice and in developing a critical pedagogy for empowerment.

## NOTES

1. Philip Corrigan, "The Politics of Feeling Good: Reflections on Marxism and Cultural Relations," (unpublished paper, Ontario Institute for Studies in Education, 1987), p. 6.

2. Sheila Rowbotham, "What Do Women Want? Woman Centered Values and the World as It Is," *Dalhousie Review,* 64 (Winter 1984–1985):650.

3. Peter McLaren, *Schooling as a Ritual Performance: Towards a Political Economy of Educational Gestures and Symbols* (New York and London: Routledge and Kegan Paul, 1986).

4. For a similar analysis of this position, see Peter McLaren, review of *God's Choice: The Total World of a Fundamentalist Christian School,* by Alan Peshkin, in *American Journal of Education* (forthcoming).

5. David Lusted, "Why Pedagogy?" *Screen* 27 (September-October 1986):3.

6. Mikhail Bakhtin, *The Dialogic Imagination,* trans. Caryl Emerson and Michael Holquist (Austin: University of Texas, 1981), pp. 293–94.

# Critical Educational Theory

SINCE THE EMERGENCE of the women's movement in the late 1960s, academic disciplines in all fields have been subjected to various levels of feminist critique and analysis. This broad feminist movement has influenced education along two lines. First, existing curricula and classroom practices have been criticized for their sexist biases and patriarchal attitudes. These critiques have addressed such questions as sex role stereotyping, the absence of women in history textbooks, the ways in which women have been portrayed in children's readers and literature, the ways in which girls have been led into certain areas of the curriculum and away from others. The second major impact of feminism on education has been the development of women's studies courses and curricula for both colleges and high schools by women teachers influenced by feminist ideas and attitudes. Women teachers have created courses addressing women and history, psychology, literature, and other disciplines; they have sought less authoritarian relationships in the classroom and are still in the process of a developing a feminist pedagogy. In the generally more conservative climate of the 1980s, some of these feminist courses and programs have come under attack at the college and university level. (Brooks and Sievers, 1983; Pollack, 1985) In high schools, feminist teachers, like all progressive teachers, are struggling against the increasingly technocratic control of public schools, a greater reliance on standardized testing, and a public cry for "the basics" in education. Nonetheless, feminist teachers in both colleges and high schools have achieved a great deal and continue to fight for progressive and feminist goals.

An impressive amount of feminist work in both curriculum and pedagogy has been achieved in the last fifteen years and is ongoing. But precisely because the contemporary feminist movement is of such recent origin, we have not yet begun to consider the ways in which feminists and feminist ideas may have affected actual practice in schools. Particularly lacking are ethnographic and qualitative studies investigating the impact of feminist ideas on teachers and students. In other words, we don't know what is happening in schools in which feminist teachers are actively critiquing and analyzing sexism in texts and the media, teaching the history of women, or discussing such issues as sexual harassment in their own and students' lives or in the schools themselves.

It was to address these questions that I decided to investigate the beliefs and practices of women high school teachers and administrators who have been touched by feminism. As a feminist and a teacher I know that women teachers of my generation are struggling with feminist issues in our own lives and in our teaching. But most feminist analyses of sexism in school texts and practices have not acknowledged the existence of this active struggle on the part of teachers. So in part, this is meant to be a descriptive study, intended to document both the achievements of feminist teachers and the obstacles facing them. This study can thus be read from a feminist perspective, as evidence of women's struggles and achievements.

This study is focused on the lives and work of women teachers, but the questions it raises about the nature of teaching and learning are part of a wider argument about schools. Thus it can be read in the context of arguments and theoretical concerns other than those of feminism alone. In this work I have been deeply influenced by two theoretical traditions: what I have called critical educational theory; and feminist theory. This is intended to be more than simply a descriptive study; my concern is to integrate a qualitative investigation with theoretical analysis. This theoretical analysis raises the question of the connection between schools and class interests, patriarchy, and race. It attempts to locate individual struggle and action in relation to larger economic and social forces. Writers about schooling, particularly in the United States, have tended to be deeply suspicious of theoretical studies. We still are drawn to the pragmatic, and suspect new and difficult (often difficult because it is new) terminology and abstract argument. This distrust of abstract theory can be valuable, particularly when we are faced with some of the more abstruse concepts in social theory. But a critical and pragmatic stance should not lead to a rejection of all theoretical analysis. That rejection can leave us limited in our ability to analyze the relationship between the actions of individuals and the social totality which has so profoundly shaped and influenced them.

In order to get beyond merely listing texts and practices or simply describing everyday life, educators in particular need a theory that can place human action and consciousness in an historical and social context. We need to be able to encompass both individual consciousness and the ideological and material forces that limit and shape human action. Critical social theory, which is often written at a very high level of abstraction, is foreign to much educational analysis, particularly that carried out in the United States. But a clearly articulated theoretical perspective is necessary in order to understand the empirical data gathered through observation and to come to a deeper understanding of society, and individuals acting within it. Only by understanding the complexity of social forces can we begin to transform them. In the first two chapters I discuss a number of theoretical approaches and begin to explore the ways in which they can be integrated into a theory that can address the quite complex issues of the relationship of gender and class on the one hand, and structural forces and human agency on the other.

The two theoretical traditions that underlie this study are the critical educational theory that has been developed in what, in Britain, has been termed the new sociology of education, and, in the United States, radical educational theory, and feminist social and cultural theory. As I will explain, both of these traditions are concerned with the critical analysis of society, and both encompass opposing theoretical approaches: (1) those which emphasize the *reproduction* of existing social, gender, and class relationships and (2) those which emphasize agency and the *production* of meaning and class and gender identities through resistance to imposed knowledge and practices. Both feminist theory and critical educational theory reflect the tensions inherent in the contradictions between these two approaches. However, there are significant differences between the concerns of feminist and critical educational theorists.

While critical educational theorists have been concerned with the production and reproduction of class through schooling under capitalism, feminist theorists have been concerned with the production and reproduction of gender under a system of patriarchy.[1] There has been little work using these two traditions to examine the production and reproduction of gender through the process of schooling itself. On the one hand, feminist theory has not really concerned itself with the impact of schooling, focusing more on early childhood (Chodorow, 1978; Dinnerstein, 1976), the relationship of patriarchy and capitalism in terms of work and class structure (Eisenstein, 1979; Kuhn and Wolpe, 1978), or on sexuality (deBeauvoir, 1961; Millet, 1970). On the other hand, critical educational theory has, with some significant exception in the work of English theorists (Arnot, 1982; Deem, 1978, 1980;

Wolpe, 1978; Spender and Sarah, 1980), simply failed to consider the question of gender to any serious extent at all. Despite these differences, both critical educational theory and feminist theory share an underlying concern with the relationship between the individual subject and an oppressive social structure. Both demonstrate the tensions between paradigms of production and reproduction as theoretical approaches. And both emphasize that social structures and knowledge are socially constructed and thus are open to contestation and change.

In order to address the relationship of gender and schooling adequately, a synthesis of these two perspectives—critical educational theory and feminist theory—is needed. Neither is adequate on its own. While critical educational theory has largely failed to recognize sexism as a significant issue to be addressed and as a result has failed to consider the ways in which gender has been both produced and reproduced through texts and material practices, existing feminist analyses of schools have too often failed to recognize schools as sites of ongoing struggle over both knowledge and social relationships. They have not revealed the ways in which feminist teachers are engaged in critical and self-conscious feminist work. Studies are needed which acknowledge critical teaching as part of an active, ongoing struggle in schools. We also need analyses of the ways in which gendered subjects are shaped through the experience of schooling, and in which the complex interaction of conflicting subjectivities and the power of gender, race, and class is made clear. This present study is meant to be a contribution to that project. Thus this study has two goals: one is descriptive, to document the lives and work of feminist teachers in urban schools; the other is theoretical, to contribute to the ongoing debate about schooling in contemporary capitalist societies. In these first two chapters I outline the nature of this theoretical debate and the competing and conflicting perspectives within it. In this chapter, I turn to critical educational theory, a theoretical perspective which has emerged in Britain, the United States, Canada, and Australia in the years since the publication of Michael Young's *Knowledge and Control* in 1971.

## CRITICAL EDUCATIONAL THEORY

It seems useful at the outset of this discussion to distinguish what I have called critical educational theory from traditional educational theory. In general, traditional educational theory has taken the existing arrangement of society as given, not changeable in any serious way, and desirable. For traditional educational theorists, schools have been seen as the means of rationally distributing individuals in what is conceived as a basically just society. Reforms are seen as adjustments of a fundamentally sound system of the social allocation of human beings. (Dreeben, 1968; Tyler, 1950; Tannner and Tanner, 1980) This traditional approach has dominated studies of schooling in the United States. When schools are criticized (and they are increasingly blamed for everything from drug use to the success of Japanese industry), it is because they fail to achieve their unstated but assumed function of reproducing and maintaining an idealized vision of U.S. society, one in which everyone finds his or her proper place: the inadequate fail and the deserving and talented rise on their merit.[2]

Critical educational theory, as its name implies, rests on a critical view of the existing society, arguing that the society is both exploitative and oppressive, but also is capable of being changed. It is at the same time more critical and more utopian than traditional educational theory. Most critical educational theorists have been deeply influenced by various Marxist traditions, although not all the theorists I have included under this rubric would claim to be Marxists. Educational theory can be divided not only into these two rough groupings; it can also be divided into two groups based on the paradigms of reproduction or production. These theoretical traditions are complex; in the rest of this chapter I will discuss their strengths and weaknesses. At the outset of this discussion, this diagram may help to clarify these relationships:

## SOURCES OF EDUCATIONAL THEORY

|  | **Traditional** | **Critical** |
|---|---|---|
| ***Production Theories*** | Phenomenology | Marxist critical theory |
|  |  | Gramsci |
| ***Reproduction Theories*** | Functionalist sociology | Structuralist Marxism |
|  | Positivism | Althusser |

What I hope this figure makes clear is not only the variety of philosophical and sociological traditions influencing educational theory, but also the complex relationships among different approaches within educational theory. Thus critical reproduction theorists share certain methodological assumptions with traditional functionalist educational theorists, and critical production theorists influenced by Marxist critical theory share certain assumptions with non-Marxist phenomenologists. However, what essentially defines critical educational theory is its moral imperative and its emphasis on the need for both individual empowerment and social transformation. That is, it emphasizes the need to develop critical consciousness in students as well as the need to change society as it is presently arranged. This study lies in the tradition of critical educational theory. Before I turn to a discussion of gender and feminist educational theory, I want to clarify the underlying paradigms of production and reproduction as they exist in critical educational theory. These concepts will be central to my later analysis.

## REPRODUCTION THEORY

Reproduction theory in general is concerned with the processes through which existing social structures maintain and reproduce themselves. Recent theorists have attempted to distinguish between two forms of reproduction: social reproduction—that is, the reproduction of class structure; and cultural reproduction—the reproduction of class cultures, knowledge, and power relationships. (Willis, 1982; Giroux, 1981) Social reproduction theory can best be seen in the work of Althusser (1971) and Bowles and Gintis (1976), while cultural reproduction theory has been more influenced by the French anthropologist Pierre Bourdieu (1977) and the English linguist Basil Bernstein (1977). While these theorists focus on different aspects of schooling, all share the underlying view that students are shaped by their experiences in schools to internalize or accept a subjectivity and a class position that leads to the reproduction of existing power relationships and social and economic structures. Despite recent criticism, which I will address later, social reproduction theorists have influenced critical eductional theory profoundly by calling into question and making problematic the role of schools and the process of schooling.

The impetus for much of early social reproduction analysis of schools, particularly in England, was the publication in English of Louis Althusser's seminal essay, "Ideology and Ideological State Apparatuses," in 1971. The work of Althusser, a French Marxist and structuralist, was both influential and controversial in the mid 1970s. (Anderson, 1980; Thompson, 1978) In "Ideology and Ideological State Apparatuses," Althusser directly addressed the role of schools in the reproduction of capitalist society, and for critical educational theorists, this essay seemed to provide the basis for a more rigorous analysis of the role of schools in capitalist societies. The key problem, as Althusser presented it, was to understand the reproduction of class relationships and the process through which members of a society accept as "real" their class identity and relationship to the means of production. In order to approach this problem, Althusser employed two key concepts: ideology and the subject.

Although Althusser accepted the ultimate importance of the economic sphere "in the last instance," he broke with earlier Marxist theory in his rejection of a simple model of an economic base and ideological superstructure which work in tandem—economic stimulus, ideological response. Instead, Althusser argued for the relative autonomy of what he called ideological state apparatuses (ISAs), those institutions through which ideology is transmitted. But although Althusser viewed these ISAs as diverse and relatively autonomous, he believed they still reflected in some ultimate sense a ruling ideology. The problem for Althusser was to explain the ways in which these ISAs function in order to reproduce class relationships and an acceptance of the existing class structure as both inevitable and unchangeable. He addressed this problem by proposing a definition of ideology which is both material and conceptual and which is embedded in and transmitted through institutions. Althusser presents two theses to explain what ideology is: "THESIS 1. Ideology represents the imaginary relationships of individuals to their real conditions of existence" and "THESIS 2. Ideology has a material existence." (Althusser, 1971, pp. 162-165) Ideology thus seems to be the cultural world that people inherit; it is imposed upon them through material practice. Their ideological views of the world, their "imaginary relationship" to the real conditions of existence, is a reflection of their actions (practices) which are governed by the structure of institutions (ISAs) through ritual, custom, lines of authority, and so forth. Thus:

> It therefore appears that the subject acts insofar as he is acted by the following system (set out in order of its real determination): ideology existing in a material ideological apparatus, prescribing material practices governed by a material ritual, which practices exist in the material actions of a subject acting in all consciousness according to his belief. (Althusser, 1971, p. 170)

The most important source of material and ideological practices for Althusser was the school. It is through instruction and social relationships in the school that students learn a way of being in the world and a view of social reality that in Althusser's sense create the subject.

The appeal of Althusser's work for critical educational theorists concerned with questions of knowledge and power is apparent. In "Ideology and Ideological State Apparatuses," Althusser was dealing directly with questions of social reproduction through the schools. In his analysis, the schools become the primary means through which subjects themselves are created. (As he says elsewhere, it is ideology which "interpellates," or creates the subject.) Moreover, Althusser's analysis locates schools within the context of a wider critique of capitalist society. His analysis appears to open the way for a deeper understanding of the ways in which schools function according to the logic of ideology and the state in capitalist society.

Despite the initial impact of Althusser's work on critical educational theory, the rather serious shortcomings of his approach were quickly evident. (Giroux, 1983) As has often been pointed out, Althusser's work provides no way to consider the subject as an agent of change and never provides a theory of consciousness. Moreover, his treatment of schools is more descriptive than analytical. He deals with schools at such a high level of abstraction that he never provides any analysis of what may actually occur in the lived relationships within the schools themselves. His theory leaves no room for a consideration of the ways in which individuals actually negotiate or resist imposed meanings. Althusser seems to provide a way to approach the vexing question of why individuals appear to acquiesce in their own subjugation and how the class structure of advanced capitalist society reproduces itself, but on closer examination, his work in many ways seems to echo the structural functionalism of traditional educational theory. For Althusser, as for the functionalists, social reproduction is a relatively smooth process of structures and apparatuses, unconcerned with the erratic or impassioned actions of flesh-and-blood human beings.

Equally influential in the development of a social reproduction theory of education was Bowles and Gintis's *Schooling in Capitalist America*, published in 1975. In this work, Bowles and Gintis represented schools in industrial capitalist societies as the means of reproducing a stratified work force whose members accepted their class position and who learned appropriate work discipline. Bowles and Gintis's work emerges from a tradition of Marxist political economy and analyzes the schools' role in relation to the reproduction of a labor force necessary to specific stages of capitalism. While they pay lip service to the idea that individuals can strive to change this system, the main thrust of their argument is to present schools and schooling as determined by a primary economic cause. Specifically, they argue that what is learned in schools corresponds to what is needed in the work place. As they put it:

The educational system helps integrate youth into the economic system, we believe, through a structural correspondence between its social relations and those of production. The structure of social relations in education not only inures the student to the discipline of the work place, but develops the types of personal demeanor, modes of self-presentation, self-image, and social class identifications which are the crucial ingredients of job adequacy. (1975, p. 131)

Thus for Bowles and Gintis the structural characteristics of schooling reproduce the existing class structure by preparing students to be workers at various levels and in various relationships of production. Despite the influence of their work, they have been criticized for the fundamentally reductionist and mechanistic nature of their argument and their failure to deal with resistance, consciousness, or change. Moreoever, Bowles and Gintis assume throughout their work that the youths they are describing are male and the social relations learned refer exclusively to the class structure and waged work. There is no recognition of patriarchal relationships in schools or the production of gendered subjects either in terms of sexual relations or patriarchal work relations. (Arnot, 1982)

The works of both Althusser and of Bowles and Gintis have been criticized for their failure to consider actual processes by which social reproduction is achieved. This criticism has been leveled by later theorists who have concerned themselves with the reproduction of class cultures and forms of knowledge through an analysis of school curricula and practices. This approach, which has been called cultural reproduction theory, is best represented by the work of Basil Bernstein (1975) and Pierre Bourdieu (1977). Both Bernstein and Bourdieu have addressed the ways in which schools legitimate certain groups through the language, knowledge, and patterns of interaction which are sanctioned as "proper" and valued. Although these theorists, like Althusser and Bowles and Gintis, focus on the role of schools in reproduction, their emphasis is on the ways in which class structure is legitimated and reproduced through variable access to knowledge and the use of language. Both Bernstein and Bourdieu operate at a high level of theoretical abstraction; neither of them describes schools as actual sites of cultural reproduction and neither really considers the possibility of resistance or contestation on the part of either students or teachers.

The goal of Bourdieu's analysis has been to unravel the ways in which the process of legitimation takes place, using the key concept of "cultural capital" to explain the functioning of the school system. In *Reproduction in Education, Society and Culture*, Bourdieu and his associate Jean-Claude Passeron refer to cultural capital as the knowledge and modes of thought that characterize different classes and groups, with some forms of cultural capital having a higher "exchange rate" than others. In the case of advanced capitalist societies, those children whose subcultural knowledge most nearly matches the valued knowledge of the educational system will tend to be most successful. Bourdieu and Passeron argue that valued school knowledge is, in fact, the cultural knowledge of the bourgeois class. Thus the children of the dominant classes appear to be successful in school because of their natural intelligence, whereas in reality they rise because they *already know* what is valued. Instead of looking at students as individuals who succeed or fail because of their own unique talents, Bourdieu and Passeron argue that we must look at students as members of class cultures who succeed or fail because of their possession of cultural capital that they accumulate because of their class membership. The fact that schools maintain a neutral stance, employing elaborate testing procedures, qualifying requirements, etc., allows them to remain relatively autonomous from the power and class structure of existing society. Bourdieu and Passeron argue that the school's "relative autonomy enables it to serve external demands under the guise of independence and neutrality, i.e., to conceal the social functions it performs and so to perform them more effectively." (1977, p. 178)

In many respects Bernstein's work analyzing language use in relation to class is similar to the work of Bourdieu and Passeron. He also is concerned with the role of schools in cultural reproduction and has worked closely with Bourdieu and his associates at the Center for European Sociology in Paris. But Bernstein separates his work from that of Bourdieu, distinguishing Bourdieu's concern with the "*structure* of reproduction and its *various* realizations" from his own concern with the "*process* of transmission." (Bernstein, 1975, p. 11) Bernstein introduces the categories of classification and framing to analyze the transmission of knowledge in schools. These classification and framing relationships, which control the organization and transmission of knowledge, "then generate distinctive forms of social relationships and thus communication, and through the latter initially, but not necessarily finally, shape mental structures." (Bernstein, 1975, p. 11) Through the transmission of knowledge in what Bernstein calls codes, certain knowledge is legitimated and made accessible to students. Bernstein argues that school knowledge and language is middle-class language, which he characterizes as an elaborated code. Working-class children, whose language Bernstein characterizes as a restricted code, are at a disadvantage in formal schooling situations, since knowledge is transmitted to them in both a language and organization that is foreign to them. Thus for Bernstein, as for Bourdieu, different class language and knowledge lead to different educational paths; schools, by employing and legitimating the language and culture of the existing dominant groups, act to reproduce existing class structure.

The work of Bernstein and Bourdieu has generated controvesy, both because of the implication that working-class language and knowledge may in fact be inferior (although both Bernstein and Bourdieu deny they intend this) but also because they both present an implicitly functionalist view of schooling. In both of their approaches, schools reproduce class structure in a relatively unproblematic way, although Bernstein's elaborate linguistic scheme can hardly be called simple. Neither Bernstein nor Bourdieu addresses the actual experience of schooling or teaching; in both accounts students and teachers are presented as passive parts of the process of reproduction. Despite the criticisms of both Bernstein and Bourdieu for their failure to address questions of gender, feminist educational theorists have employed the concepts of both cultural capital and codes in a consideration of the production and reproduction of gender in schools. Once again, although the validity of applying these kinds of analyses merely by replacing "class" with "gender" is questionable, it has been argued that these approaches, if used critically, can be applied to the social construction of gender through language. (Bisseret, 1979)

## THEORIES OF PRODUCTION

While theories of social and cultural reproduction have contributed a great deal to critical educational theory, they have come under increasing attack for their failure to address the complexity of individual experience and the absence of any consideration of resistance, agency, or change in their depiction of schools. These criticisms can be found in a variety of sources, which I want to call loosely theories of production. Production theorists are concerned with the ways in which both individuals and classes assert their own experience and contest or resist the ideological and material forces imposed upon them in a variety of settings. Their analyses focus on the ways in which both teachers and students in schools produce meaning and culture through their own resistance and their own individual and collective consciousness. These theorists of cultural producton—such as Willis (1977), Giroux (1981; 1983), Simon (1982), and Connell and his associates (1982)—are concerned in varying degrees with the social construction of knowledge and the ways in which dominant forms of language and knowledge can be critiqued and made problematic. In this they continue a theme in educational theory that can be traced back to the essays in Young's *Knowledge and Control* (1971). However, the approach of the more recent cultural production theorists differs from the earlier phenomenologically influenced theorists of the 1970s in significant ways.

In the early 1970s, theorists steeped in the tradition of phenomenological sociology developed theories of knowledge which emphasized the social construction of knowledge and the arbitrary nature of much that was taken for granted in the schools. This phenomenological critique was part of a wider movement within sociology to question the usefulness and political implication of positivism.[3] In the writings of these "new sociologists of education"—beginning with Young (1971) and Keddie (1971)—the phenomenological sociology of Schutz and Berger provided the basis for an analysis of classroom knowledge and social relationships. Central to the work of these sociologists was a rejection of positivist sociology and a demand for a return to the lived experience of social actors themselves. But while the early work of these new sociologists of education in England was valuable for its questioning of accepted definitions of knowledge and classroom relationships, too often it seemed to assume that once the socially constructed nature of knowledge was recognized, material reality and power relationships would be transformed. This analysis emphasized the production of meaning, but ignored the ideological and material forces of reproduction. As Geoff Whitty puts it, "the overemphasis on the notion that reality is socially constructed seems to have led to a neglect of the considerations of how and why reality comes to be constructed in particular ways." (1977, p. 43) The failure of the phenomenological new sociologists of education to consider the nature of social and economic power and the ways in which individuals are controlled and shaped by material as well as ideological forces left them open to severe criticism by theorists influenced by the reproduction theory of Althusser, Bowles and Gintis, and Bourdieu.

While sharing an emphasis on people's ability to make meaning, critical educational theorists concerned with cultural production should be distinguished from these earlier phenomenologically influenced theorists. Perhaps referring back to the table above, which outlines these various theoretical traditions, will clarify this relationship. Both approaches emphasize human agency and the production of meaning and culture, but the critical production theorists ground their work on a moral imperative, what Bates has called a "political commitment to human betterment." (Bates, 1980, p. 81) Moreover, the critical production theorists recognize the power of structural determinants in the sense of material practices, modes of power, and economic and political institutions. Unlike the more voluntarist phenomenological new sociologists of education, the critical educational theorists remain accutely aware that, as Marx notes, "while men [sic] make their own history, they do not make it just as they please." (1971, p. 437) Their recent work has focused in different ways on the need for a theory that will recognize both human agency and the production of knowledge and culture and will at the same time take into account the power of material and ideological structures. This dialectic between individual consciousness and structural determinants has led them to seek more developed theories of ideology, hegemony, and resistance, and to the development of what has been called "critical ethnography." (Simon, 1983) The work of the critical production theorists has been influenced by a variety of intellectual traditions, among them the Frankfurt school of Marxist critical theory, the cultural theory of Raymond Williams, the work of the Centre for Contemporary Cultural Studies at the University of Birmingham, the educational theory and practice of Paulo Freire, and the work of the Italian Marxist Antonio Gramsci. I want to turn first to Gramsci, whose work in many respects is the richest source for a theoretical approach that can encompass both agency and structure.

Gramsci was both a theorist and an activist, and dedicated his life to the struggles of the Italian working class; his arrest and eleven-year imprisonment made him a revolutionary martyr in the 1930s. The publication of *Selections from the Prison Notebooks* in English in 1971 and the subsequent translations of his earlier works have led to his recognition as a major Marxist theorist. (1971; 1985) Gramsci has been increasingly influential in critical educational theory because of his analysis of consciousness. Although Gramsci was concerned with the ways in which individual consciousness is constituted through ideological means, he never lost sight of his assertion that consciousness is capable of critique and transformation. Thus the central focus of his theoretical work is just this question of structural determinism and the possibility of human self-consciousness, critique, and action that is of greatest concern to critical educational theorists. Moreover, Gramsci's concerns were always educational in the broadest sense, as Walter Adamson points out. (Adamson, 1980) Central to Gramsci's thought is a concern with thevarious ways in which the dominant classes in any society impose their own conception of reality on all subordinate classes, and the possible ways in which the oppressed can create alternative cultural and political institutions to establish their own understanding of oppression in order to oppose and change it. Gramsci addresses these problems through the concept of hegemony.

Gramsci uses the concept of hegemony to analyze the interface of social control with various institutional structures and with a wider sense of cultural values and attitudes that go beyond the conscious control of ideas. As Boggs puts it, "hegemony can be defined as an 'organizing principle' or world view (or combination of world views) that is diffused by agencies of ideological control and socialization into every area of daily life." (1976, p. 39) This sense of hegemony as control has led to a reading of Gramsci in which every individual is "shaped" through hegemonic ideas and historical circumstances. (Mouffe, 1979) But a closer reading reveals an insistence in Gramsci's work on the power of individuals to contest hegemonic control and the resultant need for dominant classes to struggle to reimpose an hegemony in constant danger of being resisted and contested by subordinate classes. In this sense, Gramsci's thought is always profoundly anti-deterministic and always maintains an "absolute secularization and earthiness of thought" grounded in his early experiences with peasant and working class culture and his commitment to the working class as a potentially revolutionary force made up of flesh and blood individuals. (Adamson, 1980, p. 129)

As Adamson has pointed out, Gramsci uses the term hegemony in two ways—sometimes in terms of "gaining legitimate consent within the functional universe of civil society" which is the sense he uses when he argues that the working class has to struggle to achieve hegemony before it can truly achieve a revolutionary state; and sometimes as a bourgeois control of consciousness. (Adamson, 1980, p. 10) Gramsci does not imply that individual consciousness was completely dominated by the hegemonic ideas of the ruling class, or that this was possible or desirable, even in the case of eventual revolution. Quite the contrary:

> The personality is strangely composite; it contains Stone Age elements and principles of a more advanced science, prejudices from all past phases of history at a local level and intuitions of a future philosophy which will be that of a human race united the world over. (Gramsci, 1971, p. 324)

This complex consciousness, which Gramsci terms common sense, contains not only hegemonic ideas and residual,historically generated concepts, but also contains self-critique or the possibility of self-critique and hence the possibility of historical change through thought and action. This is what Gramsci means when he emphasizes that every person is a philosopher and that any true philosophy must emerge from common sense.

> The starting-point of critical elaboration is the consciousness of what one really is and in 'knowing thyself' as a product of the historical process to

date which has deposited in you an infinity of traces, without leaving an inventory. (Gramsci, 1971, p. 326)

To achieve this "critical elaboration" one must become a philosopher, not a philosopher of bourgeois abstractions, but what Gramsci called an "organic intellectual," one whose philosophy emerges from an understanding of the common sense world and the historical and economic forces which have shaped it.

Gramsci's discussion of the role of intellectuals and the need for organic intellectuals is central to an understanding of his educational thought. For Gramsci:

> Every social group, coming into existence on the original terrain of an essential function in the world of economic production, creates together with itself, organically, one or more strata of intellectuals which give it homogeneity and an awareness of its own function not only in the economic, but also in the social and political fields. (Gramsci, 1971, p. 5)

Thus although "all men are intellectuals . . . not all men have in society the function of intellectuals." (Gramsci, 1971, p. 9) Gramsci argues that in any society certain individuals will serve what is essentially an ideological function of articulating and transmitting the dominant ideas that justify the social, economic, and political structure of that society. However, societies are not homogeneous, but contain competing classes; the dominant intellectuals will be the transmitters of the hegemonic ideology of the dominant class. Their function is obviously of great importance, since they are the key functionaries who both create and transmit the specific conceptions of the world and the values of the hegemonic ideology which is to some extent incorporated into the consciousness of all classes. If the consciousness of all individuals in society is, as Gramsci says, "strangely composite," it is clear that the ideological development of personality is the result of learning and experiences in all sorts of settings—the family, church, school, work, informal associations. However, the ideological consciousness of the intellectuals is formed not primarily through informal institutions, but through the formal apparatus for the transmission of ideology—that is, through the schools. Thus for Gramsci, "the school is the instrument through which intellectuals of various levels are elaborated." (Gramsci, 1971, p. 10)

It is within the context of Gramsci's theory of hegemony and the need to establish counter-hegemonic institutions that we can understand his concern with both formal education and the alternative institutions through which the organic intellectuals of the working class can be developed. It is essential for Gramsci that these organic intellectuals remain true to their consciousness of "real forms of life," that is, that they retain a true perception of their relation to the means of production and can express an accurate understanding of their own experience within the context of class experience. In his own life, Gramsci sought the counter-hegemonic institutions in which organic intellecuals could develop in his own involvement in the *club di vita morale* in Turin and in the publication of the journal, *Ordine Nuovo*. (Adamson, 1971, p. 27) Later, he advocated the reorganization of the Italian school system and the creation of a common school, which would make critical education open to all. (Gramsci, 1971, p. 27) The goal of all these projects was to provide the site in which organic intellectuals could gain access to a common heritage and the intellectual tradition which was at present closed to them:

> The common school, or school of humanistic formation (taking the term "humanism" in a broad sense rather than simply in the traditional one) or general culture, shall aim to insert young men and women into social activity after bringing them to a certain level of maturity, of capacity for intellectual and practical creativity. . . . (Gramsci, 1971, p. 29)

The curriculum of this common school would "provide the basis for the subsequent development of an historical dialectical conception of the world, which understands movement and change. . . ." (Gramsci, 1971, p. 34) Thus central to Gramsci's conception of education is the recognition that the present is the result of struggles in the past and that a truly critical education is the development of an understanding of historical genesis in order to understand the present.

Despite Gramsci's concern with hegemony and with the power of dominant groups to shape the consciousness of subordinate groups, he insisted on the active, critical quality of consciousness and therefore on the enormous possibilities inherent in the act of schooling.

> The learner is not a passive and mechanical recipient, a grammaphone record—even if the liturgical conformity of examinations sometimes makes him appear so. The relation between these educational forms and the child's psychology are always active and creative, just as the relation of the worker to his tools is active and creative. (Gramsci, 1971, p. 42)

It is this insistence that individuals are not passive and that learning is not mechanical that distinguishes Gramsci's view of consciousness and which provides the basis for a view of schooling as a site for the production of knowledge and an interaction between the individual student and teacher that is creative. Although he recognizes individuals as historical products, he also recognizes the active quality of their being.

While Gramsci emphasizes that hegemonic control is never complete and that the process by which hegemonic ideology is incorporated into consciousness is complex and in need of analysis, some later theorists have appropriated the concept of hegemony solely as a moment of domination. Michael Apple, for example, uses the concept of hegemony to illuminate what he calls the "mechanisms of domination." (Apple, 1979) Apple's use of hegemony is still focused on the attempt to analyze reproduction—in this case, the domination of our consciousness so that we come to accept as given the social "reality" we have received. The focus of his analysis is to investigate the ways in which that hegemonic ideology is reproduced through the institutional apparatus of the schools. Thus, although he uses Gramsci's terminology, in fact he shares the emphasis on the reproduction of subjectivities and class structure of such reproduction theorists as Althusser and Bourdieu.

Recently it has been argued that the term hegemony has been employed to replace a thorough analysis of specific texts, sites, and practices. (Wexler and Whitson, 1982; Gitlin, 1979) In this usage, hegemony becomes both overpowering and static, as something successfully imposed by a ruling class on subordinate groups. But if we return to Gramsci's use of hegemony, we see that in his formulation, hegemony is never complete, always in the process of being reimposed and always capable of being resisted by historical subjects. In this sense, it becomes a theoretical tool which can be employed in detailed textual analysis and ethnographic investigation. I have discussed Gramsci's educational thought in some detail here because I feel in many ways he provides the richest source for a theory of educational production. His writings on education and his development of the concept of hegemony provide a rich source for both radical theory and practice. His analysis of the power of hegemonic ideas to shape consciousness coupled with his unshakable belief in the power of critique and political activism allow us to begin to see individuals as both shaped by history and shapers of history.

It is useful at this point to mention the work of another theorist whose work has also been dedicated to praxis—Paulo Freire. While Freire's literacy work is arguably the most influential educational work in terms of practice of the twentieth century, particularly for the non-Western world, he has not been adequately appropriated in the tradition of critical educational theory. Like Gramsci, Freire is committed to a belief in the power of individuals to come to a critical consciousness of their own being in the world. Central to his pedagogical work is the understanding that both teachers and students are agents, both engaged in the process of constructing and reconstructing meaning. Freire's literacy work in Brazil, Chile, and Guinea-Bissau—societies emerging from specific historical experiences of colonialism and imperialism—rests on the recognition of each individual's ability to appropriate reality through naming, reading, and thus knowing that reality. (Freire, 1971; 1973; 1985) From this appropriation, action can be taken and reality can be transformed. As Freire says:

> a critical reading of reality, whether it takes place in the literacy process or not, and associated above all with the clearly political practices of mobilizing and organizing, constitutes an instrument of what Gramsci calls counter-hegemony. (Freire, 1981, p. 11)

For Freire, this process involved teaching literacy to peasants through group discussion of the realities of their own lives. A part of this method is to challenge directly the received vision of reality of the church and the landlord, which teaches the peasants passivity and fatalism. Thus, Freire's literacy work is based on a critique of hegemonic ideology and the establishment of a counter-hegemony through a critical reading of both the word and the World.

One of the most important pedagogical tenets for Freire is the need for teachers to respect the consciousness and culture of their students and to create the pedagogical situation in which students can articulate their understanding of the world. At the same time, teachers must be self-reflective and seek to understand their own presuppositions and assumptions, the ideological prism through which external reality is sorted and understood. (Freire, 1973, p. 56) Thus both students and teachers must seek to understand the forces of hegemony within their own consciousness as well as in the structured, historical circumstances in which they find themselves. Freire bases his literacy work on a method of codification, through which the key words on which literacy is built emerge from the life experiences of students themselves. This method of codification and dialogue rests on his recognition that both students and teachers are subjects, creators of meaning and members of cultural worlds, and both are engaged in the task of understanding their own consciousness and the world. For true education to take place, there must be a dialogue between two subjects, as Freire says, "mediated by the world." (Freire, 1973, p. 76) In this emphasis on dialogue and on the ability of the individual to both read and change the world, Freire can provide the basis for what we might call critical as opposed to reproductive pedagogy.

The concept of hegemony has been central to much critical educational theory, and both Gramsci and Freire have been cited by theorists seeking to develop a theory of cultural production. Recently the concept of resistance has been put forward as a means of addressing the complexity of the individual's experience of social reality and the production of meaning. As adopted by the critical educational theorists of the late 1970s, the concept of resistance was used to highlight the complexity of the relationship of individal consciousness and structural determinants. This "resistance theory" has been deeply influenced by the work of critical sociologists and cultural theorists, particularly those associated with the Centre for Contemporary Cultural Studies (CCCS) at the University of Birmingham in England. Numerous studies have appeared in the last decade which summarize the collective work emerging from the CCCS. (Hall and Jefferson, 1976; Clark, Crichter, and Johnson, 1979; Hall, Hobson, Lowe, and Willis, 1980) This movement in sociology rejected earlier theories of deviance as an explanation of youthful antiauthority subcultures. Instead, the studies emerging from the CCCS argued that actions and cultural patterns that have been labeled deviant can be viewed instead as acts of resistance by individuals and groups against a dominant culture that has exploited and devalued them. Dick Hebdidge, for example, has argued that the spectacular subcultures, such as the mods, skinheads, and punks in England, represent the collective production of cultural meanings from the images and signs littered about by the dominant commercial culture of capitalism. (Hebdidge, 1979) In this view subcultures become the site of the active production of meaning in opposition to the hegemonic ideology of the dominant groups in society.

In education, the work of these critical sociologists has been particularly influential in the study of counter-school cultures. Best known and most influential of these studies is Paul Willis's study of working-class boys, *Learning to Labour*. As a research fellow at the Centre for Contemporary Cultural Studies, Willis clearly has been influenced by their collective work. *Learning to Labour* used the concept of resistance to explore the complex interaction of agency and structure. In his ethnographic study, Willis uncovered some of the mechanisms by which class culture is reproduced and the ways in which working-class boys both resisted hegemonic ideology and power and ironically helped reproduce it. Willis's interest was in the process through which working-class identity is reproduced in the individual and the group so that it is lived in the sense of being recreated and applied to new situations. In *Learning to Labour*, Willis studied a group of working-class boys, "the lads," who rejected the official ideology of the school and who actively resisted the values and knowledge they saw as being imposed upon them. Through an examination of this working-class subculture, Willis unraveled the ways in which what he calls "partial penetration" of the social structure—the lads' recognition that the school's presentation of their future as a free and open competition is a lie—led the lads not to political consciousness and attempts at emancipation, but to an acceptance of their own submission. Moreover, the lads' central recognition that manual work is in itself productive and to be celebrated was distorted by their rejection of mental work as destructive *in itself.* (Willis, 1977, p. 56) Thus the lads were relegated to the lowest status jobs in society by their own acts of resistance. In rejecting the emptiness of credentials and technocratic mental work, they also rejected analysis itself and an understanding of their place in advanced capitalist society. Without this critical understanding, the lads could only understand part of their oppression, and in fact came to accept hegemonic definitions of reality.

Basic to the lads' culture was an assumption of the inevitability of the class structure; in fact, they celebrated class as much in their own way as did the dominant groups. In this celebration, they recognized the reality of class but failed to recognize the fact that class is an historical relationship that is not inevitable. They celebrated the very real strengths of working-class culture, but they failed to turn these strengths toward emancipation. Thus despite their rejection of bourgeois cultural forms, the lads accepted the naturalness of the present system of production and could conceive of resistance as nothing but a rejection of the dominant values and knowledge, and in fact rejection of the process of abstract knowing itself. While Willis's ethnographic description went far beyond the mechanistic and highly abstract reproduction theories of Althusser and Bowles and Gintis, his work has been criticized for ultimately focusing on domination and the reproduction of class society rather than those moments of individual consciousness and class action which could provide the basis for change. In his account, resistance leads indirectly to the reaffirmation of hegemonic control.

Willis's relatively uncritical presentation of the patriarchal, sexist attitudes of the lads has brought him under criticism from feminist critics. (McRobbie, 1980) In an attempt to respond to these critiques and to respond to criticisms that in the long run his description of the lads' resistance is a sophisticated variety of reproduction theory, Willis later attempted to clarify his analysis of the relationship between individual agency and structural determinants. (Willis, 1981) Willis argues that the starting point for an investigation of the interface of the individual and the social should be the cultural sphere, "in material practices and productions, in lives in their historical context in the everyday span of existence and practical consciousness." (Willis, 1981, p. 49) Although Willis's discussion is not completely clear on this point, he seems to see this moment of cultural production not as specifically individual, but as collective, as the expression of class experience and its relationship to economic and political institutions. For Willis, the weakness of previous theories of social reproduction is that they have been concerned with "only general features of relationship," with the subsequent danger of functionalism and the absence of any theory of consciousness or agency. Willis argues that focusing on the sphere of cultural production (assuming an adequate understanding of the reality and power of the labor process, the state and its institutional apparatuses, and material determinants) will lead to a clearer understanding of the ways in which society is reproduced. (Willis, 1981, p. 50) What is significant here is the emphasis on individual and collective action and resistance:

> We can provisionally say that *Cultural Production* designates, at least in part, the creative use of discourses, meanings, materials, practices, and group processes, to explore, understand, and creatively occupy possibilities. (Willis, 1981, p. 59)

While Willis provides valuable emphasis on the production of both meaning and relationships, it is nonetheless still true that the goal of his analysis is to understand the process of social reproduction, rather than to investigate the possibilities for social transformation or ways in which theory might lead to intervention and new practices. This criticism is particularly true of Willis's defensive rejection of feminist critiques of *Learning to Labour.*

Despite the criticisms that have been directed against it, Willis's work has been important in developing concepts of resistance and cultural production in critical educational theory. The concept of resistance emphasizes that individuals are not simply acted upon by abstract "structures" but negotiate, struggle, and create meaning of their own. An increasing body of ethnographic research has used this concept as a starting point. But a wholehearted embrace of the concept can lead to predictable excesses; the political content of actions in opposition to established authority can be ignored, and virtually any act of opposition can be labeled resistance, without considering the quality of that resistance or the implications of these actions. It is clear that for the concepts of resistance and cultural production to be useful, they must be clarified and more carefully defined. The two American theorists most concerned with creating a critical theory of education which can go beyond resistance and reproduction theories are Michael Apple and Henry Giroux. (Apple, 1979; 1982; Giroux, 1981) In Giroux's work in particular, there is an attempt to apply Marxist critical theory to the question of schooling and an attempt to clarify and expand the concepts of ideology, resistance, and hegemony.

Giroux's early work analyzed and criticized the positivist problematic that underlies most educational theory; from an analysis of technocratic rationality and the sociological functionalism that still informs much curriculum theory Giroux has moved to an attempt to create an educational theory that can address the schools both as the means of social and cultural reproduction and as sites of the production of individual subjectivities and class cultures. Increasingly he has turned to the Marxist tradition of critical theory to ground his approach. Giroux is particularly concerned to demonstrate the dialectical nature of social reality, in particular what Anthony Giddens has called the "structuration of structures." (Giddens, 1979) This concern with "structuration" reflects a belief in the agency of individuals to react to and act upon the social world they inhabit, and thus insists upon the possibility of social transformation through political action or praxis. In his earlier work, Giroux rejects the correspondence theory of Bowles and Gintis and the reproduction theory of Althusser as overly deterministic and in essence a kind of Marxist functionalism. (Giroux, 1981) More than other educational theorists, Giroux has been concerned with a theory that can take into account human needs and depth psychology; in this he is deeply indebted to Marcuse and the Frankfurt school of critical theory. Most recently, he has attempted to develop a theory of ideology that can provide the theoretical basis for investigating both educational texts and practices and the role of schools in a way that "takes seriously the issues of agency, struggle, and critique." (Giroux, 1983)

Giroux's discussion of ideology is complicated, and in fact it is central to his argument that ideology itself is contradictory, existing, as he argues, in a "complex nexus of structured needs, common sense, and critical consciousness." (Giroux, 1983, p. 18) He emphasizes the possibilities of critique and agency in this view of consciousness but at the same time recognizes the reality of material forces and structural determinants on both ideology and the possibilities of practice. As Giroux puts it:

> In other words, ideology has to be conceived as both source and effect of social and institutional practices as they operate within a society that is characterized by relations of domination, a society in which men and women are basically unfree in both objective and subjective terms. (Giroux, 1983, p. 19)

Giroux's contention that ideology exists in the depths of the individual psychology in a structure of needs leads him to call for a pedagogy that takes as central the inner histories and experiences of the students themselves. Such a radical pedagogy must seek to change "subjectivity as it is constituted in the individual's needs, drives, passions, and intelligence, as well as changing the political, economic, and social foundation of the wider society." (Giroux, 1983, p. 22) But ideology also exists in what Giroux, following Gramsci, calls the realm of common sense. Common sense refers to the level of everyday consciousness with its amalgam of unexamined assumptions, internalized rules and moral codes, and partial insights. The realm of common sense is open to critique because of the hegemonic ideology it partially embodies; but common sense itself provides the means of that critique through its own thought processes and practical activities. Thus the contradictions of everyday life and consciousness itself can become the focus of a radical pedagogy. Central to Giroux's discussion of ideology is his insistence that ideology also implies the capacity for critical thinking and a transformative consciousness. In many ways, this is the most important single assumption in Giroux's formulation, since it is upon the belief in each person's ability to understand and critique his or her own experience and the social reality "out there" that any project of pedagogical and ultimately social transformation rests.

In the recent ethnographic studies of R. W. Connell and his associates in Australia, and of Roger Simon and his group in Canada, we see attempts to use more developed theories of cultural production to examine schools as social sites. (Connell, Dowsett, Kessler and Aschenden, 1982; Simon, 1983) In both cases, the concern with social reproduction has not been completely discarded, but it has been combined with an interest in the consciousness and complex realities of students and teachers moving on the material and ideological ground of schools. In both of these projects, there is an increased concern with gender as a component of subjectivity and an emphasis on the interaction of family, school, and work in the constitution of consciousness. In the project of Connell and his associates, groups of working-class public-school students and ruling-class private-school students were studied in the context of both home and school. Both class and gender were employed as central categories and an attempt was made to reconcile structural determinants and individual choice and action. What is significant here is the recognition of Connell and his group that the concept of reproduction is inadequate to explain the contradictory forces at work in schools as what he calls "processes of class" combine with or contradict "processes of gender." Moreover, Connell and his associates recognize along with Althusser that schools are "relatively autonomous" institutions, in which much more complicated interactions occur than simple and reflexive class reproduction. As Connell and his associates put it, "If 'reproduction' predominates in a given case, it is because that side of things has won out in a contest with other tendencies, not because it is guaranteed by some sociological law." (Connell, Dowsett, Kessler, and Aschenden, 1982, p. 190)

Simon and his group at the Ontario Institute for Studies in Education have embarked on an ambitious project to study the interrelatonship of school and work by looking at a group of students in vocational educational programs. Central to their study is the question of how working-class students are affected by their experiences at home, work, and school. For Simon, as for Connell and his group, it is of central importance to recognize the contradictory nature of schools and the existence of what Simon calls "moments that not only express the basic contradctions of our society, but also foster the questioning of existing social forms and a raising of alternative possibilities." (Simon, 1983, p. 254) Simon also calls for attempts at intervention through building upon the contradictions of working-class experience and schooling. His own group is attempting to create curricular materials with the goal of encouraging students to reflect upon and mediate their own experience. Both Connell and his associates and Simon and his group have developed promising approaches for a critical educational theory that takes into account paradigms of both production and reproduction; both consider gender as a significant component of individual subjectivities.

**CONCLUSION**

I have discussed the complex tradition of critical educational theory in some detail in this chapter in order to make clear the implications and value of both production and reproduction theory and to introduce some of the key concepts guiding this study. It is important to acknowledge the intended role of schools as apparatuses of social reproduction and sites of cultural reproduction at a high level of theoretical abstraction; we need to keep in mind the relationship of schools to the wider society and to recognize the realities of class and gender relationships in terms of power and control. But at the same time, the acts of resistance, negotiation, and contestation of individuals in the production of meaning and culture must also be recognized. In moving toward a theory that will capture the role of schooling in the production of gendered subjects, we have to integrate both strands of the critical tradition in educational theory with a more fully developed theory of gender in an examination of the lived experiences of teachers and students in schools. Studies of both the nature of educational knowledge as it is embedded in texts and the production of meaning and culture through lived relationships and practices need to be undertaken.

This study of feminist high school teachers employs such concepts as resistance, the production of meaning, and hegemony to investigate and analyze individual action within the bounds of structural constraints. But this study is also grounded in feminist theory. In examining the work of feminist teachers as "gendered subjects," I draw upon the work of those feminist theorists who have addressed the role of schools in reproducing inequality and oppression of women and those who have revealed the resistance of girls and women teachers in schools as patriarchal institutions. In the next chapter, I turn to an examination of this emerging feminist analysis of gender and schooling.

## NOTES

1. The term patriarchy has been the focus of considerable debate among feminist theorists. It has been criticized as imprecise and too broad for analytic usefulness by some theorists; these theorists have argued for a more limited use of the term to refer specifically to historical formations in which father-right exists as the dominant power in family relationships. Here, however, I use the broader definition, despite the difficulties, of the more universal power and privilege of men in society. In this I follow Adrienne Rich's use: "By [patriarchy] I mean to imply not simply the tracing of descent through the father, which anthropologists seem to agree is a relatively late phenomenon, but any kind of group organization in which males hold dominant power and determine what part females shall and shall not play, and in which capabilities assigned to women are relegated generally to the mystical and aesthetic and excluded from the practical and political realms." (Rich, 1979, p. 78)

2. The spate of official reports on the state of public education in the U.S. and the numerous academic studies of high schools in particular that emerged in the early and mid 1980s rest on this view of the role of schooling in U.S. society. See the National Commission on Excellence in Education, 1983; Task Force on Education for Economic Growth, 1983, for example.

3. Positivism has dominated much social science research in the twentieth century. Essential to a positivist approach is a view of human beings and social relationships as following laws similar to those governing the natural world. It assumes that knowledge of the social world is made up of objective "facts" that are open to measurement and control. Both phenomenologists and Marxist critical theorists have provided critiques of positivism. See Giroux, "Schooling and the Culture of Positivism" (in Giroux, 1981) for a good analysis and critique of positivism in educational theory.

# 2

# Feminist Analyses
# Of Gender And Schooling

IN THE FIRST chapter, the two underlying paradigms of critical educational theory were summarized. Reproduction theories of schooling were opposed to more recent analyses which argue the need to take into account human agency and the production of meaning and resistance in schools. In this chapter I turn to feminist analyses of the relationship of gender and schooling. Just as I placed this study within the general framework of critical educational theory, in this chapter I want to locate the study within the context of feminist studies of gender and schooling. There are a variety of feminist approaches to this question, approaches emerging from more general liberal feminist, radical feminist, and socialist feminist work.[1]

This study has been most influenced by socialist feminism, and I think it is important at the outset to distinguish this form of analysis from liberal feminist theory, which underlies much of the work on sex-role stereotyping in schools.

Much of the work that has been done to date on the relationship of women and schooling has emerged from liberal feminist analyses of schools. Such work has focused on sex stereotyping and bias. Theorists working from this perspective have outlined and exposed the sexual bias in curricular materials and school practices. Their focus has been on the reform of both texts and practices and on state policies toward education. Both classroom ethnographies and analyses of textbooks have emerged from this tradition.[2]

This liberal feminist work has been extremely important in documenting the biases and distortions of texts and the sexism that underlies such practices as course and career counseling for girls and boys. But it also has significant shortcomings in its narrow focus on texts and institutional structures. It has tended to ignore the depth of sexism in power relationships and the relationship of gender and class. Because this approach fails to place schools and schooling in the context of a wider social and economic analysis, it does not analyze the constraints under which the process of schooling actually takes place. Moreover, the liberal approach omits any class analysis and thus ignores not only differences between middle-class and working-class girls and women, but ignores the oppression and exploitation of working-class boys as well. As Arnot comments:

> This literature does not search too deeply into the class basis or the inequality of opportunity which boys suffer. . . . The implication then appears to be that girls should match the class differentials of educational achievement and access to occupations which boys experience. Equality of opportunity in this context therefore appears to mean similar class-based inequalities of opportunity for both men and women. Or, one could say, equal oppression. (Arnot, 1982, p. 68)

While the strength of the liberal perspective lies in its documentation of gender discrimination and the analysis of specific sexist texts and practices, its lack of social or economic analysis limits its ability to explain the origins of these practices or the ways in which other structures of power and control affect what goes on within schools. Its lack of class analysis leads to a blurring of what actually happens in schools as individuals are described only in terms of their gender and are not viewed in terms of their class or race location as well.

In the liberal feminist studies of sex-role stereotyping, there has been an implicit assumption that changes of texts and practices will lead to changes in social relationships and that girls and boys will then be equal within capitalist society. Implicit in this view is the concept that sexism exists within the realm of ideas, and that if those ideas are changed, then social relationships will also change. Such a view ignores the constraints of the material world and the various forms of power and privilege that work together in a complex and mutually reinforced process to make up social reality as we know it. It also ignores the complexity of consciousness and the existence of ideology and culture. Thus while liberal feminist critiques of sex-role stereotyping in school texts and descriptions of classroom practices have been very useful, they are of limited analytic value in investigating the complexity of the social construction of gender in the intersection of school, family, and work.

In this chapter, I examine the work of feminists influenced by socialist feminism and by critical educational theory who have investigated the relationship of schooling and gender. This critical feminist educational theory begins with certain assumptions that distinguish it from liberal feminist studies. The first assumption is that schooling is deeply connected to the class structure and economic system of capitalism; thus one focus of this work is on the relationship of women's schooling and women's work. The second assumption, again derived from more general socialist feminist theory, is that capitalism and patriarchy are related and mutually reinforcing of one another. In other words, both men and women exist in interconnected and overlapping relationships of gender and class—and, as feminists of color have increasingly emphasized, of race as well.

These theorists share the difficulties of other socialist-feminist theorists who attempt to fuse Marxism and feminism. They are deeply influenced by traditional Marxist theory, and want to apply that theory to the situation of women. But Marx and Engels were primarily concerned with the mode of production and relationships of production in class and not in gender terms. For Marx and Engels as well as for later Marxist theorists, women's oppression was subsumed within their class position and was analyzed through examining the demands of capital. Socialist-feminist theorists have argued that this traditional Marxist analysis is inadequate to reveal the nature of women's experience and oppression. (Jagger, 1983; Hartsock, 1983; Eisenstein, 1979) As Kuhn and Wolpe comment, "much marxist analysis, in subsuming women to the general categories of that problematic—class relations, labour process, the state, and so on, fails to confront the specificity of women's oppression." (Kuhn and Wolpe, 1978, p. 8) This theoretical debate, what Hartmann has called "the unhappy marriage of socialism and feminism," is complex and still being worked out. The immediate task for socialist feminists is to create a synthesis of these two lines of analysis, to create a theory that can relate what Rubin has called "the sex/gender system" and the economic system through an analysis of the sexual division of labor and an understanding of the intersection of these two forms of power. (Barrett, 1980; Eisenstein, 1979; Rubin, 1975) As Hartmann puts it:

> Both marxist analysis, particularly its historical and materialist method, and feminist analysis, especially the identification of patriarchy as a social and historical structure, must be drawn upon if we are to understand the development of western capitalist societies and the predicament of women within them. (Hartmann, 1981, p. 191)

These arguments are complex and as yet incomplete. The historical development of socialist feminism itself has recently come under scrutiny and the question of its future development is hardly clear. (Barrett,

1980; Ehrenreich, 1984; Rowbotham, Segal and Wainright, 1981; Tax, 1984) But while the relationship between socialism and feminism, capitalism and patriarchy is filled with tension, as Ehrenreich writes, a socialist and feminist perspective is still needed:

> Socialist—or perhaps here I should say Marxist—because a Marxist way of thinking, at its best, helps us understand the cutting edge of change, the blind driving force of capital, the dislocations, innovations, and global reshufflings. Feminist because feminism offers our best insight into that which is most ancient and intractable about our common situation: the gulf that divides the species by gender and, tragically, divides us all from nature and that which is most human in our nature. (1984, p. 57)

This study of feminist teachers is grounded in this complex and developing tradition of socialist feminist theory. But I have also been influenced by a variety of feminist theorists who have concerned themselves with the relationship of gender and schooling and who have approached these questions from less clearly defined theoretical perspectives.

In discussing ongoing feminist work on the relationship of gender and schooling, I have identified the same two perspectives that I used in discussing critical educational theory in general: theories of social and cultural reproduction and theories of cultural production and resistance. But I want to make clear at the outset of this discussion that this division is in certain ways artificial and should not be taken as connoting a rigid separation of these theorists into competing schools of thought. What I have identified in their work are tendencies, a concern with certain problems, a way of defining what is significant or causal in looking at the relationship of gender and schooling. What I think we can see here is what Althusser calls the "problematique" of theory—that is, the underlying questions that define what is significant and therefore what is to be investigated. I feel this distinction between those concerned with social and cultural reproduction and those concerned with cultural production and resistance is a valid one. But in a field of inquiry as new and fluid as this one, in which feminist scholars are in the process of generating theory, there will be a blurring and shifting of perspectives as the theorists themselves develop and refine their own concerns.[3]

The earliest of these investigations into gender and school from a critical feminist perspective can be found in what I have called feminist reproduction theory. Feminist reproduction theory is concerned with the ways in which schools function to reproduce gender divisions and oppression. In response to this emphasis on reproduction, a smaller but growing body of work has emerged which employs the concepts of resistance and cultural production to look at the lived experience of girls in schools. Most recently, the concept of counter-hegemony has been raised as a way of approaching the politically conscious work of teachers. These theoretical traditions focus on different moments in the experience of girls and women in schools, and as I have emphasized, it should be kept in mind that these categories are a kind of heuristic device, and that the individual theorists themselves may be engaged in their own process of growth and reconceptualization. But trying to clarify and identify their underlying theoretical assumptions can be of help to all of us as we attempt to generate theory and focus our own research.

## FEMINIST REPRODUCTION THEORY

Although socialist feminist theory has developed rapidly in the last decade, work that explicitly addresses the role of schools in reproducing gender oppression has been somewhat limited. The most significant work has emerged in England, and has been influenced by the work of both new sociologists of education and Marxist theorists who have focused on the role of schools as ideological state apparatuses. While these feminist reproduction theorists take somewhat different approaches, they all share a common belief in the power of material historical analysis and a focus on the relationship of class and gender. Basic to their approach is the view that women's oppression in the paid workforce and in domestic work is reproduced through what happens in the schools. Thus statistical analyses of women's inferior position in the economy are tied to sexist texts and discriminatory practices in schools. Official state educational policies are examined for their overt and hidden assumptions about women and their "proper" role in the economy. The major focus of this approach is on the connection between sexist practices in the schools and women's oppression in society as a whole.

Feminist reproduction theorists are deeply influenced by traditional Marxist analysis and have been primarily concerned with social reproduction—that is, the reproduction of relationships to and control over economic production and work.[4] These theorists are concerned with the nature of women's work, both within the public sphere and within the domestic or private sphere. Thus the focus of their analysis is on the class-based nature of women's experiences in schools and the ways in which the experience of schooling reproduces gender oppression. But they also emphasize the differences between middle-class and working-class experience of gender. For them, what are being reproduced are not simply "men" and "women," but working-class or bourgeois men and women who have particular relationships to one another and to production which are the result of their class as well as their gender. As Arnot comments, this approach reveals "the diversity of class experience and the nature of class hegemony in education." (Arnot, 1982, p. 69)

The debate about the relationship of gender and class underlies the work of all of these feminist reproduction theorists who concern themselves with schooling. While they recognize the "specificity" of women's oppression and often speak of patriarchal as opposed to class oppression, they remain committed to the primacy of production. Because of the centrality of this sphere of material life and production in their thought, feminist reproduction theorists see the relationship between gender as an ideology and women's role in production as fundamental to any analysis of women and schooling. Thus for them, work, both paid and unpaid, becomes the central focus of analysis. Since they are concerned with the role of schooling in the reproduction of existing society, they focus on the way schools work ideologically to prepare girls to accept their role as low paid or unpaid workers in capitalism.

Several socialist feminist analyses of reproduction and schooling are also deeply influenced by the work of Althusser. This is particularly true of the work of Michelle Barrett. An Althusserian perspective in this case implies an emphasis on the "relative autonomy" of schools as sites of ideological reproduction. The most obvious difficulty of using an Althusserian approach for an analysis of gender is that Althusser is concerned with the category of class, not gender, and there is some question whether it is fruitful or even possible to substitute "gender" for "class" in this analysis. However, Althusser's insistence that ideological apparatuses are "relatively autonomous" from the economic sphere appears to provide the means to raise questions of gender and patriarchal practices apart from, although not unrelated to, questions of class and capitalist practices. Barrett recognizes the complexity of this issue and argues that the method of analysis must include an analysis of gender *within* specific class structures. (1980) While feminist theorists of schooling influenced by Althusser provide a more complex view of the role of schools in relation to women's oppression in capitalism, they remain focused on the question of how this oppression is reproduced and, like Althusser, argue at a very abstract level of analysis that leaves little room for human agency or resistance. While a view of schools as ideological state apparatuses "relatively autonomous" from the economic base provides room for the contradictions and disjunctions evident in schools, it still remains within a paradigm of reproduction. The strengths and weaknesses of feminist reproduction theory may be clarified if we look at the work of several representative theorists.

AnnMarie Wolpe was one of the earliest socialist feminists to address the role of gender in schooling. Her work includes both a critique of official government statements on education and a critique of earlier work on sexism in schools for its lack of economic or social analysis. One of the strongest parts of Wolpe's argument is her attack on what she calls "stratification" theories, which look at women's position as the result of innate psychological differences such as lack of aggression, excessive anxiety, or orientation toward "intrinsic" rewards such as nurturing relationships. (1978, p. 306) Wolpe argues that such interpretations fail to recognize the powerful forces of the capitalist economy with its need for unpaid domestic work and a reserve army of labor.

Wolpe reveals in detail the ideological assumptions about the role of women in society which underlie the offical British Norwood (1943), Crowther (1959), and Newsom (1963) reports and the later unofficial Conservative Green and Black papers (1977). Wolpe shows clearly the acceptance of the role of women as wives and mothers doing unpaid work in the home and the failure to recognize either that women *do* work in paid jobs or that the paid work that they do is in low-paying and dead-end jobs. Thus by failing to recognize the reality of women's actual work as paid workers and by encouraging girls to see their own work (both paid and unpaid) as insignificant, Wolpe argues that these reports perpetuated and helped to reproduce existing inequality. She argues that in influencing school policies, these reports have played a vital ideological role in reproducing the oppression and subordination of women in the economy.

This kind of analysis is valuable since it points to the connection between hegemonic ideological views (in the consciousness of the groups—primarily men—who wrote these reports) and actual educational policy and practices as they are carried out in the schools. But what Wolpe does not address is precisely *how* these assumptions and views are put into practice in the schools or how students and teachers have accepted, incorporated, or resisted them. This is not to discredit or discount Wolpe's analysis, but to point to the limitations inherent in a view of ideology as the uncontested imposition of a view of reality or set of values. Wolpe's tendency to depict the imposition of ideology as a relatively smooth and almost mechanical process is the result of her focus on reproduction at a very abstract level of economic and structural analysis. It is Wolpe's reliance on reproduction and her failure to address the question of human agency that ultimately limits her work. While she criticizes stratification theories of education for their failure to provide any economic analysis of the role of schooling, she accepts without much criticism social reproduction theories of education. As she says:

> I want to consider the educational system first, as a mechanism of *reproduction* of "agents" in the sense that it operates, more or less successfully, to qualify them both "technically" and ideologically; and second, as a mediating agency in the *allocation* of agents into the division of labour. (Wolpe, 1978, p. 313)

Since Wolpe is concerned with women and women's oppression, the use of this reproduction paradigm ultimately leads her to depict schools as the means of reproducing women who will accept their role as workers in both paid and unpaid work. The ideology of the school is seen as important in justifying this role both for those who control the educational system and for the girls and women in the schools.

Wolpe's approach shares the limitations and shortcomings of all social reproduction theory, as we saw earlier in a discussion of the work of Bowles and Gintis and Althusser, in that it fails to address individual consciousness or the possibilities of resistance, but it also fails to address forms of women's oppression other than those of work. Wolpe later qualifies her early, rather functionalist, view by referring to the "relative autonomy" of schools. Following Althusser, she sees schools as mediating between students and the demands of capital. This "relative autonomy" recognizes the contradictions involved in the relationship between the economic base and the schools. Nonetheless, Wolpe's central concern remains the reproduction of women in relation to work. Thus, Wolpe's analysis has no place for sexuality, human needs, the historical and class-based forms of resistance of women, or the contradictory role of schooling for girls in a system of patriarchy. Ultimately Wolpe's work is valuable in pointing out the need to locate women's oppression and women's experience in schooling within a larger social structure and in making central the role of work in women's lives, but at the same time her work is frustrating in its tendency toward a mechanical form of reproduction theory.

Another early influential feminist analysis of schooling was Rosemary Deem's *Women and Schooling* (1978). In this general overview, Deem combines quantitative information about the percentage of girls in various courses, the numbers of girls taking and passing exams, and the percentage of women in various teaching and administrative jobs. She also writes from the general perspective of social reproduction, arguing that the schools are central to the process of maintaining and reproducing the existing sexual division of labor. This underlying paradigm of social reproduction leads Deem to emphasize the significance of work and the role of schooling in preparing women for certain kinds of work. Thus she emphasizes the domestic nature of working-class girls' curriculum, with its assumption that women's primary work will be unpaid labor in the home. She also points to the small number of girls in mathematics and science, and shows how that in turn excludes women from certain university courses and later technological and professional jobs. Deem points out that the schools do not create this division, but that they reinforce the present arrangement of society through their acceptance of the status quo in both class and gender terms:

> Education does not create the sexual divison of labour, nor the kinds of work available in the labour market, nor the class relationships of society, but it rarely does anything to undermine them. (Deem, 1978, p. 20)

Deem emphasizes that schools, in their expectations of boys and girls and in their authority structures (so heavily dominated by men in positions of power and authority), transmit different cultures to boys and to girls, and that the "choices" made by students in school reproduce the existing sexual division of labor.

One of the strengths of Deem's analysis is her emphasis on the continuity of women's work as mothers in the family and as teachers in the primary schools. As she makes clear, the role of women in doing the unpaid labor of nurturing, feeding, and caring for the material needs of children is not the reflection of some innate "women's nature," but is part of the existing social division of labor in capitalism. This arrangement may not be inevitable in capitalist societies, but in the present organization of capitalism, it is central to the reproduction of the work force. Thus Deem argues that there is a continuum between the rearing and socialization of children within the family, where the primary work is done by mothers, and the socialization that takes place in the early years of schooling, with the work done by women teachers.[5] Deem's grounding in social reproduction theory leads her to reject views of women's nurturing role as either "natural" or the "fault" of women. As she emphasizes, it is the structural organization of capitalist societies that leads to this division of labor and the resulting personal and psychological traits assumed to be natural to men and women. She criticizes the view that women teachers are inadequate because of their feminine qualities or their roles within their own families:

> Furthermore, there is the implicit assumption (in criticizing women teachers) that all these factors are the fault of women and are not attributable

> to their relationship with men in the sexual division of labour, or to the
> manner in which capitalist societies organize and reward productive and
> non-productive work. (Deem, 1978, p. 116)

This emphasis on the existing division of capitalist societies in gender
as well as class terms is one of the strongest elements in Deem's work,
since it leads her to see the experiences and struggles of women
teachers in the context of larger social dynamics.

Although Deem's book provides a valuable overview of the relationship of women and schooling, its strength—a recognition of the role
of schools in reproducing an unequal gender and class system—is at
the same time a limitation. Like Wolpe, Deem fails to deal adequately
with ideology and the way in which women teachers and students
exist within a structure of socially influenced needs and desires—an
ideological world of male hegemony, in Arnot's phrase. Moreover, she
ignores the struggles and resistance of both teachers and students to
this hegemony. While her work is useful in providing specific evidence
of discriminatory patterns, the picture it gives of this process is one
sided. Again, what is needed here is an examination of the way in
which these meanings and forms of power are negotitated and worked
out in the actual lived reality of teachers and students in schools.

An interesting analysis of women's schooling from a similar perspective but in the United States context is provided by the recent
work of Kelly and Nihlen (1982). Like many other socialist feminists,
Kelly and Nihlen argue that an emphasis on paid work as the only
meaningful form of work ignores the significance of domestic unpaid
labor—a domain that has been defined as "women's sphere" in advanced capitalist societies like the United States. They argue that the
ideological assumption that this work is the responsibility (and natural
province) of women profoundly shapes women's working lives, making
certain jobs "unnatural" for women because of the difficulties involved
in doing both paid and unpaid work. Moreover, the assumption that
certain characteristics are natural to women—such as nurturance,
caring, sensitivity, etc.—leads women into certain jobs and not others.
Kelly and Nihlen consider the evidence that links schools to this
division of labor, but unlike some of the earlier writers who focus on
reproduction, they also raise the question of the extent to which
students "do in fact become what the messages of the schools would
have them become." (Kelly and Nihlen, 1982, p. 174) Thus, while they
work from the perspective of reproduction theory, seeking to delineate
the reproductive role of schools in the creation of the sexual division
of labor, they also begin to question the adequacy of that perspective
in addressing the realities of women's experience in schools.

In looking at the relationship of schooling and women's work, Kelly
and Nihlen focus on several areas of schooling. They look first at

authority patterns and staffing. Using available statistics and data, they show clearly the unequal representation of women in positions of authority and status and note the *decline* of women in higher paying and higher status jobs since the 1950s. They also examine the formal curriculum, and, citing the numerous studies of curriculum and texts that exist, particularly in the 1970s, show again the sex-stereotyping prevalent in curricular material at both the primary and secondary levels. They then examine the ways in which knowledge is distributed in the classroom itself and in the social relationships of schooling. As they point out, this area is least researched; we know the least about the ways in which girls and boys are treated by male and female teachers. But the studies that do exist point to discrimination and stereotyped expectations based not only on gender, but on race and class as well. Thus working-class girls of color receive the least attention and have the lowest expectations from teachers. On the other hand, there is evidence that teachers tend to prefer white middle-class girls to black working-class boys, for example.

The most interesting part of Kelly and Nihlen's discussion is the final section on the possible resistance of girls. As they make clear, girls do continue to higher education (although disproportionally to two-year colleges as opposed to more elite public and private four-year colleges) despite the ideological message of the school curriculum that their place is at home doing domestic work. As Kelly and Nihlen point out, women do not accept the ideological message of the school unproblematically. Instead, they obviously "negotiate" that knowledge in light of their own emotional, intellectual, and material needs:

> While the above suggests that women may not necessarily incorporate all "school knowledge" it should not be taken by any means to deny what school knowledge in fact is or its attempted transmission in the classroom. Rather, it is to point out that within the classroom sets of knowledge renegotiation and/or active filtering occurs that may counter what the schools consider legitimate. How this renegotiation occurs we do not know, yet there is ample evidence to suggest its existence. (Kelly and Nihlen, 1982, p. 175)

Kelly and Nihlen's work is valuable in pointing to the weaknesses of the reproduction paradigm and in calling for an examination of the ways in which girls appropriate or reject school knowledge about the roles of women in paid and domestic work. They point to evidence that girls do not unproblematically accept the vision of sexual identity transmitted to them through the social relationships, authority patterns, and curriculum of the schools. However, despite their valuable work in recognizing the need to take into account resistance in looking at girls in schools, Kelly and Nihlen's work has certain limitations. First, I think, is their failure to apply or develop the concept of resistance to account for contradictory relationships to schooling on the part of both students and teachers. And second, they are still tied to a theory of work and work value that does not address the sexuality and power in the relationships of men and women which are extremely important in school settings, as in all socially contructed gender relationships.

Certainly the most sophisticated and fully developed theoretical work in the socialist feminist sociology of education can be found in the work of Madeleine Arnot. A sociologist of education versed in the theories of Bernstein and Bourdieu, Arnot has developed a critique of their work and an analysis of traditional reproduction theory from a feminist perspective. Her work combines a thorough knowledge of both reproduction and resistance theory. Her use of these difficult and sometimes contradictory traditions provides a complex analysis of the relationship of gender, class, and schooling. As Arnot defines her own position: "I do not believe that one can disassociate the ideological forms of masculinity and femininity, in their historical specificity, from either the material basis of patriarchy or from the class structure." (1980, p. 60) Underlying all of her work is the central understanding that social relationships are always in process and are constructed by individual human beings within a web of power and material constraints.

While Arnot has been influenced by reproduction theory and is sympathetic to a materialist analysis, she is critical of feminist reproduction theory for its failure to deal with the question of resistance and the contested nature of the construction of both class and gender identities. Arnot argues that socialist feminist social reproduction theorists, like social reproduction theorists in general, project too total a vision of domination and oppression. In some of these accounts, girls are turned into women through the effects of schooling in a mechanical process in which their humanity and consciousness is simply ignored. Thus Arnot suggests replacing the concept of reproduction with Gramsci's concept of hegemony. As she says:

> By putting the concept of hegemony, rather than "reproduction" at the fore of an analysis of class and gender, it is less easy in research to forget the *active* nature of the learning process, the existence of dialectical relations, power struggles, and points of conflict, the range of alternative practices which may exist inside, or exist outside and be brought into the school. (1982, p. 66)

In seeking a way to address questions of cultural production, Arnot looks back to the work of Bernstein and Bourdieu. While Arnot criticizes their work for their failure to address gender, she is also deeply influenced by this work, particularly that of Bernstein and his theories of the framing and transmission of knowledge. She uses his concept of a code to suggest that "one can develop a theory of gender codes which is class based and which can expose the structural and inter-actional features of gender reproduction and conflict in families, in schools and in work places." (1982, p. 80) What this focus on gender codes would allow us, Arnot argues, is to remain conscious of the different moments and crossing structures of power which are *ne-gotiated* by individuals in social settings. Thus she emphasizes that girls negotiate and construct their own gendered identities through different definitions of what it means to be a woman from their families, their peers, the school, the media, etc., and that this involves both contradictions and conflict. Arnot argues that feminist educational theorists, by emphasizing hegemony, the existence of competing codes of meaning and the continual *process* of social relationships, will be able to unravel the complexities of the effects of both capitalism and patriarchy on individual lives without falling into the mechanical functionalism of reproduction theory or the atheoretical stance of liberal theory.

The work of Arnot and Kelly and Nihlen draws attention to the need to take into account agency and the production of meaning on the part of girls and women in schools. It also reiterates the basic argument of Barrett and other socialist feminists that we must try to understand the construction of gender within specific historical and social sites. While this project is only beginning, the basis for this investigation can be found in the work of feminists who have turned to the lived experience of girls and women in school. The most developed of this work has come from feminists using the concept of resistance to investigate the lived reality of working-class girls in and out of schools. But other work is in process and emerging that considers the lives and work of women teachers as well as students. This new work builds upon the earlier reproduction studies, but its basic focus is quite different. It is to this work that I now want to turn.

## FEMINIST RESISTANCE AND CULTURAL PRODUCTION THEORY

As we have seen, feminist reproduction theory has emphasized the ways in which schooling *reproduces* existing gender inequalities. This work has focused on the ideological function of texts and classroom practices in reinforcing patriarchal hegemony. And because much of this work is grounded in traditional Marxist class analysis, it has also focused on the connection between schooling and women's work in the paid work force. I have argued that the limitation of this approach lies in its failure to consider human beings as agents who are able to contest and redefine the ideological messages they receive in schools. It is a much too mechanistic and all-encompassing view of social reality. In response to these limitations, some feminists have begun to examine girls' and women's experiences in schools from the perspective of resistance and cultural production theories.

While traditionally the concept of resistance has been used to describe public counter-school or antisocial actions, there is an emerging view that this definition is inadequate to explain or understand the lives of girls or women. Some feminist theorists argue that resistance has different meanings for boys and for girls and that girls' resistance can only be understood in relation to both gender and class position. (Connell, 1982; Davies, 1983; Kessler et al., 1985) These theorists insist that women as well as men can resist domination and oppression and they as well as men negotiate social forces and possibilities in an attempt to meet their own needs. This is the same dialectic between human needs and human will that we see in other critical studies. Women, as well as men, are enmeshed in social relationships and ideological, as well as material, webs of meaning and power. But because they are oppressed by sexism as well as class, the form of their resistance will be different from that of men. Moreover, schooling may have a different meaning for them than it has for boys of their same class or race. As Gaskell comments:

> ... schools, operating in their traditional function, do not simply reproduce sex-stereotypes or confirm girls in subordinate positions. Certainly they do that much of the time. But they have also long been a vehicle for women who wish to construct their own intellectual lives and careers. (1985, p. 35)

Girls and women with different race and class subjectivities will have different experiences in schools. Both their resistance and their "reading" of the ideological messages of schools will differ in specific school settings. And of course girls of different class and race subjectivities will be met with varying expectations on the part of white and black, male and female teachers, depending on these teachers' own views of what is gender appropriate. By adding the categories of race and class to that of gender, we can begin to reveal the diversity and complexity of girls' and women's experiences in schools.

Among the most important work addressing the experiences of working-class girls in schools has come from feminist sociologists of education who have studied groups of antisocial or antischool girls. The work of these theorists has emerged from a wider sociological investigation of youth subcultures as the site of working-class resistance to the hegemonic ideology of capitalism. Much of this research has come from the Centre for Contemporary Cultural Studies at the University of Birmingham in England and the feminist research group there has engaged on a number of valuable projects and critiques. (Women's Study Group, 1978) While these feminist sociologists have worked closely with the male sociologists using this perspective, they have also generated sharp criticisms of this male-focused work. In particular, feminist sociologists interested in the question of working-class girls' resistance have been both influenced by and critical of the work of Willis. As we saw in the first chapter, Willis's study of working-class boys, *Learning to Labour*, made an immediate impact on critical educational theory, and particularly on critical ethnographic studies of schools. However, despite its originality and richness, it shared the weakness of earlier studies in its exclusive examination of the public subcultures of young men. This exclusive interest in men and a subsequent (sometimes subtle, and sometimes not) definition of male counterculture as working-class culture evoked a feminist response, both in the form of critiques of Willis and also in the sociological investigation of working-class girls' experiences and subcultures on the part of feminist sociologists. (McRobbie, 1980; Acker, 1981)

The feminist critique of Willis centers around two general points. First is the fundamental question of the reliability of descriptions of working-class culture by male sociologists. The question raised here is whether Willis has given weight to certain aspects of that culture because of his own ideological valuing of male actions. That is, does Willis, in common with other male sociologists, "see" male activities and spheres as significant, but remain "blind" to the significance of female spheres. This criticism follows the line of argument of feminist anthropologists who have critiqued male anthropologists for their own form of male ethnocentrism. (Reiter, 1975)

The second feminist criticism of Willis's work highlights his failure to address the sexist oppression inherent in male working-class culture. As McRobbie puts it:

> Shopfloor culture may have develped a toughness and resilience to deal with the brutality of capitalist productive relations, but these same "values" can be used internally.... They can also be used, and often are, against women and girls in the form of both wife and girlfriend battering. A fully *sexed* notion of working class culture would have to consider such features more centrally. (McRobbie, 1980, p. 41)

Thus a failure to recognize the oppressive sexism of male subcultures and an acceptance of the absence of girls in these subcultures are clearly interrelated. In fact, of course, the boys' own sexism reproduces the role of girls in working-class culture as oppressed and subordinate.

While these relationships may in some sense reflect a logic of capitalism, it is not the ideology or state policies of capitalism that directly pressures these working-class girls, but rather the immediate and oppressive sexism of working-class boys. As we will see, feminists argue that the moral failure to condemn or even to see the sexism of male subcultures leads in turn to a failure to understand the full dynamics of working-class culture and life.

In response to this feminist critique of Willis and other male work on boys' public subcultures, feminists have turned to an examination of girls' antisocial and counter-school groups. While studies of girls' subcultures are still relatively few in comparison to studies of boys', McRobbie, Fuller and others in England, and Thomas in Australia have contributed ethnographic studies that raise new questions about the intersection of gender, race, and class in the lives of working-class girls.

Studies of white working-class girls have been undertaken by McRobbie and her associates at the Centre for Contemporary Cultural Studies in England and by Thomas in Australia. These studies have been deeply influenced by the cultural production theories of Willis and others at the CCCS and provide an alternative approach to similar problems. McRobbie worked with a group of 14–16 year-old-girls at a Birmingham youth club for six months, while Thomas studied two groups of antischool or antiacademic girls—one group in a middle-class and one in a working-class school—for an academic year. In both cases, there was a clear and stated recognition that the experiences and actions of girls could not be explained solely through an analysis of class, but that, as McRobbie put it, "their culture would be linked to and partly determined by, although not mechanically so, the material position occupied by the girls in society." (1978, p. 97) Thus unlike comparable studies of male subcultures, McRobbie and Thomas begin with an awareness of the dual oppression of working-class girls through both capitalism and patriarchy. And in looking at the gender-specific nature of their oppression and their resistance, they focus on the private, domestic world of sexuality and the family as well as the public world of the street and paid work.

Both McRobbie and Thomas studied girls who rejected the values of school and official state institutions. In both cases, these girls rejected school values of propriety and behavior. They challenged dominant views of what a "proper girl" should be like by asserting the values of their own sexuality in sites where that sexuality was deemed inappropriate. Both McRobbie and Thomas emphasize the ways in which these girls use sexuality as opposition to the authority of the school or to middle-class definitions of femininity. As McRobbie comments:

> One way in which girls combat the class-based and oppressive features of
> the school is to assert their "femaleness," to introduce into the classroom
> their physical maturity in such a way as to force the teachers to take notice.
> A class instinct then finds expression at the level of jettisoning the official
> ideology for girls in the school (neatness, diligence, appliance, femininity,
> passivity, etc.) and replacing it with a *more* feminine, even sexual one.
> (1978, p. 104)

Thomas found that counterculture girls in opposition to school authority vacillated between aggressive defiance and an assertive and
sometimes coy sexuality, particularly toward younger men teachers.
(Thomas, 1980, p. 148) What these girls appear to be doing, then, is
using their sexuality as an act of resistance to accepted norms of
female behavior. They take what society tells them is their most significant characteristic and exaggerate it as an assertion of their own
individuality. Thus their aggressive use of sexuality becomes a form
of power. This use of sexuality, however, is particularly true of working-
class girls, and only in the context of situations defined by school or
state authorities. Thomas found that antischool middle-class girls
were much more likely to be immersed in the ideology of romance,
and to view marriage as a way out of the boring and irrelevant world
of school and the dead-end world of work. (Thomas, 1980, p. 152) And
working-class girls, although they would flaunt their sexuality in such
sites as schools, were in fact very cautious in entering into sexual
relationships, since they were very much aware of the dangers of
becoming labeled "loose" in the context of their own working-class
culture.

This attitude toward sexuality among working-class girls is supported by Wilson's study of "delinquent" or "semi-delinquent" girls
in a northern England working-class community. (Wilson, 1978) She
found that girls categorized themselves into three groups based on
sexual activity—virgins, one-man girls, and lays. Most of the girls categorized themselves as one-man girls, which meant they engaged in
sex, but with an ideology of romance and the intention of marriage.
For them, marriage seemed the only possible future. Thomas points
out that in the groups of antischool girls she studied, working-class
girls, although committed to marriage and in particular to motherhood, had far fewer illusions about what married life would be like.
Middle-class girls, on the other hand, were immersed in an ideology
of heterosexual romance. (Thomas, 1980, p. 152) In fact, for working-
class girls with no education and no skills, marriage is virtually an
economic necessity. Thus what the girls have to oppose to the dominant-class culture and ideology of the school and the state is the
assertion of their own exploited and submissive role in working-class
culture. Just as Willis's lads emphasize their masculinity as manual

workers and thus end up in dead-end and exploited unskilled jobs, so these girls emphasize their femininity in a traditional sense and end up exploited both in their unpaid labor in the home as well as in the marginal and low paying jobs they can get as waged workers. As Thomas comments:

> In this way, counter-school youth subcultures serve to reproduce working-class culture in the new generation; by providing a vehicle for the expression of opposition to the school's central academic purpose, they help to ensure the perpetuation of a voluntary labouring class under capitalism. (1980, p. 131)

In the case of girls, this reproduction is achieved not only through the conflict of class cultures, but within the context of patriarchal definitions of sexuality and exploitative sexual relationships that *appear* to provide girls with their only source of personal power.

Feminists have argued that a definition of working-class culture that only considers the public world of paid labor and public sites such as the pub or the street corner in fact ignores the domestic world of unpaid labor, sexuality, and childcare that is found in the private world of the family. They call for studies of girls and women that can reveal the ways in which their lives reflect the forces of production and reproduction and the ways in which they experience the social world and negotiate within it. Such studies should reveal the ways in which women's lives also reflect and are shaped by the forces of production and reproduction in different configurations but just as powerfully as men. In this way, a more complete picture of working-class culture and of the process that Willis calls cultural production would be illuminated. Such studies would approach both public and private sites, definitions of work that include both waged and nonwaged work, and an analysis of sexuality and deep human needs as they are mediated in all aspects of class culture, for both men and women.

In order to understand the totality of working-class life both for men and women it is necessary to realize that culture is produced in *both* public and private sites and that social relationships, the production of culture, and the values given to both work and individual experience are profoundly influenced by both capitalism and patriarchy in both sites. This is not to argue that the public and private are unrelated. Quite the contrary. They are deeply related and intertwined as they make up a whole cultural world. But because boys and girls, men and women, are associated in sometimes very rigid ways with one sphere or the other, they work out individual and collective cultural responses that are quite different, though at the same time complementary. The central argument here is that to ignore the cultural world of women is to distort any understanding of the *totality* of working-class culture or resistance. A focus solely on the public male world of waged work and public oppositional culture is inadequate to come to grips with the ways in which the logics of both capitalism and patriarchy structure the individual experiences of working-class men and women and their common class culture as well as their separate men's and women's cultures.

The emphasis on the production of meaning and culture in public and private sites is, I think, instructive when we turn back to the question of schooling and the nature of the resistance of girls to the school. As both McRobbie and Thomas make clear, while the official ideology of schooling for girls sometimes reinforces the messages of working-class culture, at other times it is in opposition to that culture. But the working-class girls studied by McRobbie and Thomas fall back on an exaggerated form of the definitions of gender from wider working-class culture (as well as the ideological messages of the dominant culture as expressed in advertisements and the media). Their resistance thus simply embeds them more deeply in the culture of domination and submission, of double work, both waged and nonwaged.

The concept of resistance is used by McRobbie and Thomas to address the complexity of class and gender experience of working-class girls. But that concept is also useful in examining the nature of race and its relation to gender and class. The work of Fuller is particularly interesting in raising questions about the nature and implications of girls' resistance. Fuller studied groups of Afro-Caribbean, Indo-Pakistani, and white British girls in a London comprehensive school. (Fuller, 1980; 1983) By making the category of race central to her work, she brings the realities of racism and the need to consider racial identity as well as gender and class position into her work in a fundamental way.[6]

Thus the question of cultural production and resistance takes on a more complex meaning, since these girls have to negotiate structures of what Amos and Parmar have called "triple oppression." (Amos and Parmar, 1981) Fuller explores the strategies these girls of color employ to try to gain some control over their lives. She points to three areas of control that emerged from her observation and interviews with these girls: "Firstly, their being controlled by others in and out of school; secondly, their wish for control for themselves at some time in the future; and lastly (and perhaps paradoxically) their need to exercise forms of self-control and resentment now in order to achieve self-determination later." (1983, p. 127) While Fuller has been influenced by the work of Willis and male sociological theorists of resistance, her work is more concerned with the ways in which girls, both individually and collectively, make sense of and try to negotiate oppressive social relationships and structures in order to gain more control over their own lives.

Fuller's work calls into question certain qualities of the concept of resistance that are relatively unquestioned in work that has focused on counter-school girls' subcultures. Basic to Fuller's analysis is the idea that critical understanding (what Willis would call "penetration") and the formation of an oppositional subcultural view of society is not necessarily tied to public antiauthority and counter-school groups. Instead, she argues in the case of black British girls in particular that they can combine a critical view of schools with an ability to manipulate and succeed within the school system of examinations and certification. She sees these girls' ability to combine two apparently contradictory perspectives as the result of their own social identities as black girls in a racist and sexist society. In their negotiation of these double or triple forms of oppression, the girls create complex responses. As Fuller points out:

> Indeed in regard to many aspects of their current and likely future lives some of the fifth-year girls were markedly *more* critical and politically sophisticated than most of the boys. Yet in terms of overt "symptoms" within the school the girls' opposition to what was actually and what in the future they thought was likely to be happening to them, did not come across as obviously oppositional or troublesome in the terms that others describe "troublesome" male pupils. (1983 p. 125)

Thus while the black girls were conscious of the racism and sexism they faced, they did not express that criticism as opposition to the school and the system of certification that the school represented. Instead, they overtly conformed to school mores (although in a way that was often on the edge of overt rejection of the rules) and more specifically saw the school as the means to resist the sexism of black British culture and the racism of white British culture. As Fuller puts it:

> I would suggest that in concentrating on pupils rather than on opposition we can get away from seeing pupils' cultural criticism as residing solely or even mainly in overt resistance to schooling. It may be that girls are too busy resisting other aspects of their life for resistance to schooling to have a high priority for them. (1983, p. 140)

Fuller argues that black girls saw the obtaining of academic qualifications as an assertion of their own sense of competence and intelligence that was denied them in black culture as girls. In her interviews, Fuller cites the girls' consciousness of and rejection of the sexist and sometimes sexually violent attitudes of black boys. In the face of this they asserted their own toughness and, in particular, their ability to work for wages and thus have a basis for their own identity and autonomy. They were also conscious of the double standard within their own families in which they were expected to do unpaid domestic work while their brothers were allowed and even expected to be out of the house. The success of black girls in state schools caused resentment among black boys, who saw this as a challenge to accepted women's roles. Here is Marcia, a black fifteen-year-old girl:

> I've always got my head in a book. I don't think they like it because they [black boys] are always commenting on it and they say, "You won't get anywhere," and sometimes I think they don't want me to learn or something like that, you know, but I spoke to my mum about it, and she said I shouldn't listen and I should keep working hard. (Fuller, 1983, p. 131)

This is not to argue that the sexism these black girls face is unique to black culture, or that they are not equally or more affected by racism. Fuller argues that it is in in fact the conjunction of these two forms of oppression along with their assertion of their value as girls and as blacks that gives them the anger and power to resist dominant definitions of themselves and to assert their own control over their futures by taking control of the educational system of certification and examinations:

> The conjunction of all these—their positive identity as black but knowledge of racial discrimination in Britain, their positive identity as female but belief that both in Britain and in the Caribbean women were often accorded less than their due status—meant that the girls were angry at the foreclosing of options available to them as blacks and as women. (Fuller, 1980, p. 57)

Fuller's work raises important issues not only for the study of resistance and cultural production, but also about the nature of subcultures in general. First of all, the combination of critical consciousness and an apparent acceptance of the official ideology of school success needs to be examined. Fuller argues that these girls have achieved a certain "penetration" of the ideology of certification, in that they consciously intend to use school examinations to gain some control over their lives. However, this might also be viewed as a form of individual accomodation to existing social conditions rather than a collective cultural pattern that can be called resistance. I think the question that is not addressed in Fuller's work concerns the nature of class in capitalist societies. By positing only race and gender as relationships of oppression, Fuller's black girls fail to critique the nature of work in class society and thus in one sense oppose one relationship of oppression to another in just the way Willis's lads do. That is, just as the lads use racial and sexual domination to assert themselves and thus obscure their own class oppression and the nature of the work that they will do, so these black girls use "success" in school and an acceptance of the dominant definitions of work in capitalism to oppose the racism and sexism they experience in both black and white culture. The individual manipulation of school and certification may allow them to oppose oppressive aspects of their own lives, but without a more political and public expression, it may be more individual accommodation than collective resistance.

The other question raised by Fuller's work is about the nature of subcultures in general. Because as we have seen girls are usually excluded from the public arena of the street, the subcultural groups they form are private and exist in the domestic sphere of the home or in friendship groups among girls. While the black boys in the school in which Fuller worked joined a wider Rastafarian culture and adopted the style and clothes of that subculture, the girls were excluded. Thus what Fuller calls a subculture in fact was based on a kind of common understanding and attitude toward both whites and boys and an assertion of a common pride in being black and female. While this common understanding was very significant as the girls struggled to assert their own autonomy and to gain some measure of control over their lives, it did not have the weight of more public male subcultures. What Fuller does not address is the need for a more public and politically conscious assertion of black women's identity and strength that could be the basis for more organized resistance. As Amos and Parmar state:

> Existing political organizations cannot always incorporate all these strug-
> gles and although we feel that as black women we should organize with
> other black people against the racism in this society, and as part of the
> working class we should organize around the issues of work and non-work,
> and as women we should organize with other women, as black women
> we also need to organize separately around the issues that are particular
> to our experience as black women, experiences which come out of the
> triple oppression we face. (Amos and Parmar, 1981, p. 146)

Resistance is an important concept in looking at the lives of girls and women in schools, because it highlights their ability as human agents to make meaning and to act in social situations as well as to be acted upon. However, resistance must be used with some caution and careful definition if it is to help us understand social processes. We can see some of the difficulties involved in the use of the term resistance in Anyon's work on girls in fifth-grade classrooms. Anyon's research rests on a more general and shallow study of the cultural life of younger girls. She studied one hundred students in five different schools and depended on one seemingly quite structured interview with each child. Anyon's data is rather weak in comparison with the work of Fuller, McRobbie, and Thomas, but she does raise similar issues in her theoretical discussion. Like the cultural production theorists, Anyon questions the view of ideology as complete and uncontested. Instead, she argues that girls and women do not passively accept the dominant ideology of sexism, but rather negotiate ideology and needs. She argues that "gender development involves not so much passive imprinting as *active response to social contradictions.*" (Anyon, 1983, p. 26)

Like Fuller, Anyon questions the depiction of resistance as solely found in public antisocial or counter-school actions. Instead, and following Genovese in his work on black slavery, she argues that women employ a "simultaneous process of accommodation and resistance" in their negotiation of social relationships. However, the line between accommodation and resistance is somewhat blurred in Anyon's discussion and it is not always clear when exaggerated feminine behavior or acquiescence to school authority can be viewed as accommodation or resistance. What is lacking in this work is a more rigorous discussion of what resistance might mean in complex and overlapping relationships of domination and oppression. Because Anyon does not locate the girls she interviews in a more complete social world, she is left with a description of attitudes or actions in school and must interpret them outside of a social totality. In this use, terms like resistance and accommodation become convenient categories into which observed behavior or beliefs can be slotted. Anyon's work is frustrating in this regard. Consider, for example her analysis of this incident in one of the working-class fifth-grade classrooms she observed:

> She told me that she wanted to be a veterinarian, and that she did not want to work in a factory like her mother did. I watched her persist at her desk to do her school work as the teacher screamed at the other children and gave confusing directions, and as belligerent boys roamed the classroom. Thus, I interpret her hard work not only as an accommodation to expectations that she do what is demanded in school, but also that through this accommodation she can resist both present and future social discomfort. (Anyon, 1983, p. 41)

There is something in this picture of a hostile school world ("screaming" teacher, "belligerent" boys) and the obedient, hardworking girl that smooths over the complexity of the competing forms of social power that this girl (not to mention the teacher and boys) negotiates in order to make sense of the world and to try to assert herself. I think the problem here rests ultimately in the lack of depth in our understanding of this girl, the school, the class and gender ideology that is embodied in the texts and social relationships of the school and among school children and in the dynamics of the girl's own family. In this case, the terms accommodation and resistance feel like empty generalities that can, in fact, be applied to any social action.

Anyon does make some valuable points about the need to make "resistance" cultural and public if it is to serve as the basis for social change. Like McRobbie, McCabe, and Garber, Anyon points out that individual resistance to sexism and the negotiation of existing concepts of femininity lead to an acceptance of the status quo: "While accommodation and resistance as modes of daily activity provide most females with ways of negotiating individually felt social conflict or oppression, this individual activity of everyday life remains just that: individual, fragmented, and isolated from group effort." (Anyon, 1983, p. 45) It has been argued that the failure of girls and women to participate in public antisocial groups and activities is the result of a certain psychological tendency to turn opposition and anger inward in private, self-destructive activities. (Cloward and Piven, 1979) However, it may be that girls and women resist dominant and oppressive patriarchal values and relationships, though in different ways from men. But the question for women is how the human ability to create meaning and resist an imposed ideology can be turned to praxis and social transformation.

The recent work of Gaskell (1985) and Kessler, Ashenden, Connell, and Dowsett (1985) develops the question of women's relationships to schooling by examining the activities and choices of girls and women in particular school settings. Both of these studies argue that schools are contradictory sites for girls and women and, despite the existence of sexist texts and practices, provide the possibility of resistance to male hegemony on the part of both students and teachers. Kessler et al. argue:

> Yet the central fact, perhaps the most important point our interviews have demonstrated, is that the complex of gender inequality and patriarchal ideology is not a smoothly functioning machine. It is a mass of tensions, contradictions, and complexities that always have the potential for change. (1985, p. 47)

By looking at girls and women teachers in both a working-class public school and an elite private school, Kessler et al. show the need to analyze power relations and the intersection of family and school in each particular site. They argue that we need to understand the intersection of the family, the workplace, and the state in terms of sexual ideology and structural constraints on girls and women. Thus the struggles of elite girls will be quite different from those of working-class women teachers. To ignore class and racial difference in studying gender is to distort both the realities of their experience and the possibilities for resistance in each site.

Gaskell argues along similar lines. In studying working-class girls' course choices, Gaskell argues that girls were not simply "reproduced" by male hegemony, but that they made choices according to what their own understanding of the world was like:

> They knew, for their own good reasons, what the world was like, and their experience acted as a filter through which any new message was tested, confirmed, rejected, challenged, and reinterpreted. Changing their minds would have meant changing the world they experienced, not simply convincing them of a new set of ideals around equality of opportunity and the desirability of a different world. (1985, p. 58)

Gaskell emphasizes the need to hear the girls' own stories. She argues that reproduction theories that view women as simply the creation of male hegemony or sexist institutions obscure and fail to see the realities of women's strengths and agency.

> There is ... a tradition in feminist scholarship that has emphasized that women's consciousness is not simply an internalization of male forms but contains its own alternative interpretations, commitments and connections. ... The relation between women's consciousness and man's world is complex and involves accommodation, resistance, and self-imposed and externally imposed silences. Correspondence does not account for their relationship. (1985, p. 58)

These studies point out and analyze oppressive practices and ideology, but at the same time insist that the schooling of girls is a complex process that contains contradictions and points of resistance which must be analyzed in each particular historical instance.

Throughout the feminist studies of resistance and cultural production certain themes are illuminated. First is the assertion that all people have the capacity to make meaning of their lives and to resist oppression. This is expressed in Giroux's remark that "inherent in a radical notion of resistance is an expressed hope, an element of transcendence." (1983, p. 108) Second, that that capacity to resist and to understand is limited and influenced by class, race, and gender position. People will use the means at hand, the power that they can employ to meet their needs and assert their humanity. This is clear in the work of Fuller, Gaskell, and Kessler, Ashenden, Connell, and Dowsett. Third, as is clear from the work of Willis, McRobbie, and Thomas in particular, the various "solutions" sought by people embedded in sexist, racist, and classist society can lead in fact to deeper forms of domination and the oppression of others. Willis's lads "partially penetrate" the logic of capitalism, but that rejection leads them to a rejection of mental work and to the celebration of a masculinity defined by sexism and racism. McRobbie's and Thomas's girls' rejection of school ideology leads them to a definition of their own sexuality that leads back to the oppressive sexism of working-class culture. And Fuller's girls, in succeeding in school and gaining certification, assert their abilities and value as black women, but accept the logic of work in capitalism. For women, who are so often excluded from the public sphere, the question of whether resistance can lead to change if it is only expressed in individual critique or private opposition is a very real one. And this leads back to the schools. Can schools become a possible "public sphere" for the encouragement of resistance and the building of a critical counter-hegemony for girls?

## FEMINIST TEACHING AS COUNTER-HEGEMONY

I have argued that the concept of resistance has been used as a heuristic device to explore the possibilities of human agency. But various theorists have argued that we need to expand our view of agency to include not only resistance in the form of various kinds of opposition to oppressive beliefs and practices, but also to include more critical and politicized work in the form of organized and conscious collective oppositional actions. This kind of opposition has been called counter-hegemony. By this is meant the creation of a self-conscious analysis of a situation and the development of collective practices and organization that can oppose the hegemony of the existing order and begin to build the base for a new understanding and transformation of society. Feminist counter-hegemonic teaching has been developed and refined at the university level in a variety of women's studies programs (Bunch and Pollack, 1983; Spanier, Bloom and Borovak, 1984). In these programs both feminist theory and methods have been developed to provide a counter-hegemonic vision and critique. (Bunch, 1983; Schniedewind, 1983). Teaching in public schools, although more profoundly bounded by institutional constraints, also contains the possibility of transformative work. This does not imply that this work will be achieved without enormous and sometimes overpowering opposition. As Freire says, critical teaching in dominant institutions means that teachers are constantly living a contradiction. But possibilities for critical work exist within that very contradiction. It is vital that teachers recognize not only the structural constraints under which they work, but also the potential inherent in teaching for transformative and political work. As Connell comments:

> The doctrine that tells teachers the schools are captive to capitalism and exhorts them to get on with the revolution outside, could not be more mistaken; it is teachers' work as teachers that is central to the remaking of the social patterns investing education. (1985, p. 4)

If the work of critical teachers can be viewed as counter-hegemonic work, the latent and unarticulated resistance of students can in turn become the focus of critical teaching. As Giroux points out, "the concept of resistance highlights the need for classroom teachers to decipher how modes of cultural production displayed by subordinate groups can be analyzed to reveal both their limits and their possibilities for enabling critical thinking, analytic discourse, and new modes of intellectual appropriation." (1983, p. 111) Thus the ability of students to resist and the forms of subcultural resistance become the focus of critical teaching, which can be part of the creation of a counter-hegemony.

In the second part of this book, I turn to the work of women teachers to examine both the obstacles they face and also the ways in which their work expresses the potential for transformation. As several feminist educational theorists have argued, the schools can provide the site for feminist teachers to raise issues of sexism and gender oppression. Kelly and Nihlen, for example, mention the potential significance of the women's movement in legitimating an alternative vision of gender. As they comment, "It well may be—and more research is needed—that the presence of a woman's movement provides a means of making resistance 'count' and sets the tenor for the renegotiation of knowledge within the classroom." (1982, p. 176) McRobbie and Garber have argued along the same lines that the school can be a progressive force if it can serve as a site for feminist teachers to introduce the ideas of the women's movement to girls and to open up a discussion of the structural limitations and oppression they face. (McRobbie, 1978, p. 102) Kessler et al. argue the need to "democratize the curriculum by reorganizing knowledge to advantage the disadvantaged; and to mobilize support for democratization of the schools in relation to gender, as much as other structures of power." (1985, p. 46)

This view of teaching as critical work leads us to see the resistance of students as an important basis for the building of a counter-hegemony, as teachers and students together struggle to understand the forces acting upon their lives. Many feminists have argued that feminist teaching can contribute to the building of this alternative vision of social reality and morality (Hartsock, 1979; Lather, 1984) The outline of this kind of argument can be found in the work of Lather. (1984) Lather's work has focused on the impact of feminism and women's studies courses on the education of teachers. She has argued that while male critical educational theorists speak of the need for critical teaching, they have overlooked the power of feminism to challenge the status quo through the creation of women's studies courses and critiques of sexist texts and practices. Looking back to Gramsci for a theoretical perspective to understand the work of feminist teachers, she argues that his call for a progressive social group who can create what he calls a new historical bloc can be found in the women's movement.

> Adopting gender as a basic analytic tool will enable critical theory to see what is right under its nose: the possibilities for fundamental social changes that open up when we put women at the center of our transformation. (Lather, 1984, p. 52)

In Gramsci's view, revolutionary theory had to be grounded in the struggles of everyday life. Lather argues that feminist theory and the women's movement are grounded in precisely these struggles to make the personal political. A critical, materialist feminism could illuminate these relationships of personal and public and begin to create a new politics that would be truly revolutionary. Lather applies the Gramscian concept of counter-hegemony to this feminist work. She emphasizes the difference between counter-hegemony and the more commonly used term of *resistance*. *Resistance* is "usually informal, disorganized, and apolitical," but *counter-hegemony* implies a more critical theoretical understanding and is expressed in organized and active political opposition. As Lather defines it:

> The task of counter-hegemonic groups is the development of counter-institutions, ideologies, and cultures that provide an ethical alternative to the dominant hegemony, a lived experience of how the world can be different. (1984, p. 55)

While the starting point of counter-hegemonic work is the world of students, both their oppression and their opposition, it must move beyond that point to provide more democratic relationships, an alternative value system and a critique of existing society.[7]

While feminist teaching has focused on gender oppression, we need to remember that feminists in teaching and outside of it tend to be middle class and white. Thus although they share with working-class girls the common oppression of being female in a patriarchal and sexist society, they are divided from them by class and, in the case of girls of color, by race as well. Nonetheless, the work of conscious feminists *is* important in building counter-hegemony; schools can be sites for critical teaching and work in specific sites and under certain conditions. What we need to do is to be very clear about the specific meanings of class, race, and gender for people in differing relationships of control and power in a society dominated by capitalism racism, and patriarchy. We need to locate ourselves in these complex webs of relationships and then attempt to act at whatever sites we find ourselves, in ways that will encourage both resistance to oppression and the building of a counter-hegemony through critical understanding.

In the following chapters, I examine the critical work of feminist teachers in public high schools. In so doing, I consider both agency and the structural forces acting upon these teachers in their lives. In the intersection of life histories, consciousness, and practice, we see the forms and patterns this dynamic takes. In my analysis, I employ the concepts of reproduction, resistance, and counter-hegemony that have been raised in these first two chapters in relation to women's lives. The methodoloy I have used is deeply influenced by feminism, and it is to a discussion of that feminist methodology that I turn in the next chapter.

## NOTES

1. See Jagger (1983) for the clearest and most accessible discussion of the differences among radical feminism, liberal feminism, and socialist feminism in terms of feminist theory in general.

2. Significant examples of this approach are Frazier and Sadker (1973); Levy (1974); Chetwynd and Harnett (1978); Byrne (1978); and Delamont (1980). See Acker (1982) for an overview of various feminist approaches to the question of the relationship of gender and schooling from the perspective of the early 1980s, particularly with reference to British studies.

3. Feminist inquiry into the relation of gender and schooling has continued in recent British works which have addressed the existence of sex bias in schools and have begun to focus on potential strategies to redress those practices from a variety of theoretical perspectives. *Girl-friendly schooling* (1985), a selection of papers from the 1984 conference on girl-friendly schooling, provides both studies of sexist practices and discussions of feminist intervention and policy suggestions. Weiner's *Just a bunch of girls* (1985) contributes a valuable perspective on race that has been missing from most accounts. Mahony's *Schools for the boys* (1985) presents a powerful indictment of co-education from a radical feminist perspective. Like Walkerdine (1981) Mahony raises significant questions about the nature of male sexual power and privilege that have not been adequately addressed in either liberal or socialist feminist studies.

4. Representative theorists in this tradition are Barrett (1980); David (1980); Deem (1978; 1980); Kelly and Nihlen (1982); and Wolpe (1978; 1981).

5. As Mannicom has shown, this shared nurturing role of mothers and primary teachers does not necessarily lead to mutual understanding and cooperation between mothers and primary teachers, even though sexist assumptions about the "natural" nurturing qualities of women are at work in both instances. (Mannicom, 1984)

6. See also the recent articles by Brak and Mihas (1985), Foster (1985) and Riley (1985).

7. Examples of curriculum and teaching can be found that begin to bring together feminist and critical thinking. For example, a group of radical teachers at the Group School in Cambridge, Mass. created various curricula with working-class girls. This work has been published as *Changing learning, changing lives.* (Gates, Klaw, and Steinberg, 1979) These teachers used the life experiences of working-class girls to draw out themes of race, class, and gender for critical analysis. Schniedewind and Davidson have provided a feminist curriculum for public schools in *Open minds to equality* (1983). McRobbie and her associate Trisha McCabe have published *Feminism for girls*, directed at both students and teachers and youth workers. McRobbie and McCabe raise questions of the transmission of images and values through the media and texts, both in school and outside of school. Articles in this collection critique such areas as the depiction of girls in the literature curriculum, the nature of secretarial work, and the overt and hidden meanings of *Jackie*, the British equivalent of *Seventeen.* In providing analyses and critiques of sites and texts that make up the cultural world of teenage girls, McRobbie and McCabe hope to provide these girls with the kind of critical vision that will lead them to see their experiences critically as socially created and thus open to resistance and change.

# 3

# Feminist Methodology

*If I want to define myself, I must first of all say: I am a woman;*
*on this truth must be based all further discussion. A man never*
*begins by presenting himself as an individual of a certain sex; it*
*goes without saying that he is a man.*

*—Simone deBeauvoir*

IN THE LAST chapter, I located this study within an emerging tradition of critical feminist studies of gender and schooling. Despite wide differences in approach, these studies are in some sense all concerned with class and gender as these are reproduced or produced in schools. Increasingly, women of color have made it clear that it is necessary for feminists to address the realties of race as well as gender. As I outlined in the last chapter, the ways in which these three dynamics—class, race, and gender—have found expression in individual lives and social relationships has formed the agenda for a variety of critical studies of gender and schooling, work that is still only beginning. This study of women teachers focuses on these dynamics and on the interplay of forces of social reproduction on the one hand and cultural production and resistance on the other. It is deeply influenced by both the critical educational theory outlined in the first chapter and the various critical feminist analyses of gender and schooling discussed in the second chapter.

In this chapter, I have built upon the work of feminist theorists in the social sciences who are collectively creating a feminist methodology and epistemology. In the past decade, feminists in various disciplines in the social sciences have been engaged in creating a new methodology. This methodology has developed gradually and organically from the process of women studying women in social settings, in texts, and in the media. This methodology shares the central insight expressed by de Beauvoir, that women must begin by defining themselves as women. This starting point reflects central insights about the relationship of power, knowledge and language and calls into question the intellectual tradition not only of positivism, but of Western thought from its beginnings with the Greeks. (O'Brien, 1983) Women researchers and theorists have come to see that in the dominant Western intellectual tradition, male experience is taken as the norm, as what is truly human. Women therefore by definition are either insignificant or incomplete. Thus women know who they are through a double process. On the one hand, women know themselves through the male hegemonic vision of reality, in which acting subjects are men and women are something other, what Gornick calls "women as outsider." (1971) On the other hand, women as human beings *are* subjects, and have the ability to act and to critique their own experience, even if that capacity is denied in structures of knowledge and in the language itself. Therefore women exist in a peculiar tension of both being subjects and being denied as subjects. The recognition of this dynamic has led feminists to question the ability of male thought to address and adequately comprehend the experiences of women. In response, a new methodology has been developed, one which begins with women as the referent and which as a result calls into question the methodology, assumptions, and language itself of the male intellectual tradition.

In this feminist methodology three major themes occur again and again, and all of them reflect de Beauvoir's insight that women must begin by defining themselves in a society and intellectual tradition that denies them subjectivity. First, feminist researchers begin their investigation of the social world from a grounded position in their own subjective oppression. This leads them to a sensitivity to power that comes from being subordinate. As Westcott puts it, women's consciousness is "influenced by the ideas and values of men, but is nevertheless uniquely situated, reflective of women's concrete position within the patriarchal power structure." (1979, p. 429) Thus feminists recognize that their vision of social reality and their definition of what is important emerge from their own position in society. Feminist research, like critical Marxist theory, thus rejects the desirability or even the possibility of value-free research. Instead, feminist research *begins* with the unique vision of women in a male-defined society and intellectual tradition. Secondly, feminist research is characterized by an emphasis on lived experience and the significance of everyday life. This is expressed in several different ways: by an assertion that the personal is political; by a rejection of positivism and an interest in

phenomenological or social interactionist approaches; by a new definition of the relationship between woman researcher and woman
subject. Thirdly, feminist research is politically committed. In rejecting
the possibilty of value-free research, feminists instead assert their commitment to changing the position of women and therefore to changing
society. This overt commitment to women's rights, which is shared
by women of widely ranging political views, reflects women's own
personal experiences of subjugation within a male dominated society.

This feminist methodology cuts across various political stances
within feminism. It is not without its weaknesses, noticeably when it
fails to address forms of oppression other than gender oppression.
But I want to argue that this weakness is not intrinsic to the methodology itself, but reflects a failure on the part of some feminist approaches, particularly liberal feminism, to develop a more clearly
articulated analysis of society as a whole. The methodology itself can
provide a valuable means for critical feminist researchers to begin to
address the relationship between structural oppression and the realities of individual lives. Thus a critical feminist methodology can illuminate the dual processes of social and cultural reproduction on
the one hand and resistance and the production of meaning on the
other that as we have seen is central to the tradition of critical educational theory as well as to socialist feminist theory. Before turning
to the specific nature of this study, I want to discuss in more detail
the characteristics of the feminist methodology I have employed.

First, feminists have argued that it is necessary for women to ground
our research from the beginning in a recognition of our oppression
as women in male-dominated society. This entails identifying and
articulating both objective oppression in practices and relationships
and the male blindness to women's experience, the tendency of what
Mary O'Brien calls "male stream thought" to assume that "man" implies humanity and vice versa. (O'Brien, 1983) Feminists go beyond a
cataloging of oppressive practices and sexist assumptions in dominant
male thought to examine our own consciousness. Women's consciousness is complex, including both a critical understanding of
oppression and at the same time male hegemonic ideology in both
the dominant intellectual tradition in which women have been trained
and in the language itself. (Bisseret, 1979) Women's consciousness
includes both hegemonic ideas from the male tradition and the pos-
sibilties of critical consciousness or what Gramsci called "good sense."
Before women researchers can understand the experiences and consciousness of other women we must come to understand ourselves
and the ways in which we know. In other words, women must develop
that critical consciousness or good sense that Gramsci spoke of; we

must interrogate our own consciousness, language, and ways of knowing in order to come to see the realities of our own relationships. In
this way, feminism asks for a radical reappraisal not only of practices,
but of consciousness itself.

This need to call into question our own consciousness has been
articulated by a number of feminists. Dorothy Smith argues that we
must begin at the "rupture" between our experiences as women and
what she calls "social forms of consciousness." She argues that feminist understanding should begin with the contradictions inherent in
being both "other" and a conscious acting being at the same time. As
she defines her own work:

> The disjuncture which provides the problematic of this inquiry is that
> between the forms of thought, the symbols, images, vocabularies, concepts,
> frames of reference, institutionalized structures of relevance, of our culture,
> and a world experienced at a level prior to knowledge of expression, prior
> to that moment at which experience can become "experience" in achieving
> social expression or knowledge, or can become "knowledge" by achieving
> that social form, in being named, being made social, becoming actionable.
> (Smith, 1979, p. 135)

For that world of experience prior to expression to become conscious
knowledge and thus open to understanding and change, it is necessary that we recognize the authenticity of women's subjective experience and knowledge—both our own as researchers and that of
the women we study.

The central emphasis on women's subjective experience leads to
the second characteristic of much feminist research: the importance
given to lived experience and the significance of everyday life. The
connection here is obvious. Since women have so often been relegated
to the private, domestic arena, their actions in everyday life define
them in a way that is not the case for men, who are accustomed to
defining themselves in the public arena and who exist as actors in a
world of abstract thought and concrete public action. As Dorothy
Smith puts it:

> The place of women, then, in relation to this mode of action is where the
> work is done to facilitate man's occupation of the conceptual mode of
> action. Women keep house, bear and care for children, look after him when
> he is sick and in general provide the logistics of his bodily existence. Women
> work in and around the professional and managerial scene in analogous
> ways. . . . At almost every point women mediate for men the relation be-
> tween the conceptual mode of action and the actual concrete forms on
> which it depends. (1979, 16)

Smith is making a very significant point here. She is arguing that what
has been defined as significant in male stream thought is in fact a

truncated vision of social reality, that another arena of social reality exists, made of the "actual concrete forms" of material life; this material basis for the public conceptual world of men rests on the labor of women. In order to understand the full nature of human experience, power, and action it is necessary to bring that world to light. This entails the creation of a new "naming" of women's experience. Feminist theorists argue that this cannot be achieved through the present abstract language of male theory. Instead, women must create a new language based on women's actual lived experiences. As Stanley and Wise comment:

> Our experience has been named by men, but not even in a language derived from their experience. Even this is too direct and too personal. And so it is removed from experience altogether by being cast in abstract and theoretical terms. We need a women's language, a language of experience. And this must necessarily come from our exploration of the personal, the everyday, and what we experience—women's lived experiences. (1983, p. 146)

Understanding the lives and experiences of women means becoming concerned with this "actual concrete form" of material life. Smith points out that women's place as invisible and subordinate is not simply a matter of an hegemonic language and ideology, but that women *live* their relationships in the material world. The consciousness of women is not created solely by a male hegemonic ideology or language; it is grounded in actual material life. That material life includes obligations and duties which are not only different from those of men, but which male studies of social reality have left invisible.

It should be clear that to argue the need to take seriously the everyday lives of women is not to accept as valid the dichotomy between private and public arenas as separate universes. As socialist-feminist theorists emphasize, the role of women in reproducing social life and life itself is essential to the public world of production. De Beauvoir reminds us that "women have never constituted a closed and independent society; they form an integral part of the group, which is governed by males and in which they have a subordinate place." (1961, p. 562) What focusing on the everyday life of women should do instead is reveal that connection between public and private, between production and reproduction. In socialist-feminist research, the everyday world is not a self-contained world; quite the contrary, it is an integral part of the social whole. What's more, the relationships and values of that private, everyday world are shaped by larger social and economic forces:

> The everyday world, the world where people are located as they live, located bodily and in that organization of their known world as one that begins

> from their own location in it, is generated in its varieties by an organization
> of social relations which originate "elsewhere." It is like a dance in which
> the subject participates or in which she is placed. The "shape" taken by
> the dance and the part she plays in it bring into being the dance as an
> actual organization of social relations through time. (Smith, 1979, p. 176)

Thus focusing on the everyday world reveals the ways in which larger forces, both ideological and material, place limits and conditions on our actions. But at the same time, making the everyday world of women the center of social research demonstrates that a concentration solely on the public arena is equally inadequate. Feminist scholarship, by revealing the everyday lives of women, opens up the other half of social reality which has been ignored in studies of public life. As duBois puts it, "feminist scholars are engaged in almost an archeological endeavor—that of discovering and uncovering the actual facts of women's lives and experiences, facts that have been hidden, inaccessible, suppressed, distorted, misunderstood, ignored." (1983, p. 109)

The emphasis on everyday life in feminist research is similar to phenomenological and interactionist approaches which focus on the subjective nature of knowledge and the role of the researcher in the process of research.[1] Dueli-Klein calls this method "conscious subjectivity" in which both observer and observed are acknowledged and validated. (Dueli-Klein, 1983, p. 94) Mies refers to "conscious partiality," in which the researcher identifies her own experience with the women who are the objects of her research. (Mies, 1983, p. 122) This emphasis on the conscious subjectivity of the researcher also implies a recognition of the subjectivity of the objects of research. Thus, as Westcott comments, "women as objects of knowledge are viewed not as passive recipients nor as active, conforming reflections of society." (1979, p. 428) Instead, women are recognized as subjects who have knowledge and who can act upon the world, even when their subjectivity is denied in male hegemonic ideology and language. The interaction between woman researcher and the women who are the objects of research is thus defined in a radically different way from not only positivist research, but traditional ethnographic research as well. As Oakley argues:

> A feminist methodology of social science requires that . . . the mythology
> of "hygenic" research with its accompanying mystification of the researcher
> and the researched as objective instruments of data production be replaced
> by the recognition that personal involvement is more than a dangerous
> bias—it is the condition under which people come to know each other
> and to admit others into their lives. (1981, p. 58)

Westcott describes this methodology as "the inter-subjectivity of meaning of subject and object." (1979, p. 425)

I am arguing then that an emphasis on the everyday experiences of women and the need for the researcher to locate herself in terms of her own subjectivity is fundamental to a feminist methodology. Moreover, a different kind of relationship is called for between knower and known, researcher and the object of research. Not only is this methodology based on a mutual recognition of women's subjective experience, but as Dueli-Klein points out, it also admits and employs other resources such as "intuition, emotions, and feelings both in ourselves and in those we want to investigate." (1983, p. 95) Stanley and Wise argue that an analysis of "feeling and experience in an examination of 'the personal' " should be the major focus of feminist research. (1983, p. 178) Traditional male research rejects emotion and feeling as "unscientific" and biased, assuming the possibility of a neutral, purely rational approach. (Hochschild 1975) But a feminist methodology denies that this emotionless and value-free research is possible or desirable. Instead, it asserts the human interaction of knower and known when both are human beings with knowledge and feelings and the ability to act. One of the major goals of feminist research is for both women as researchers and women as the objects of research to come to understand and explore their own consciousness and material conditions of existence through dialogue.

This leads me to the last characteristic of feminist research, which is its political commitment. The overt recognition of the feminist researcher's own subjective position, the identification of the feminist researcher with the object of her research, and the recognition of the deeply political nature of everyday life, lead feminist researchers to a commitment to changing the existing social order. Feminist theory and methodology is grounded on a commitment to praxis. This political commitment reflects the essentially materialist theory of knowledge that underlies feminist research. That is, for feminists, the ultimate test of knowledge is not whether it is "true" according to an abstract criterion, but whether or not it leads to progressive change. In this sense, feminist research simply follows Marx's famous dictum that the point is not to understand the world, but to change it.

This commitment to praxis can be seen in Dorothy Smith's call for a sociology not about, but *for* women:

> Suppose then we began to devise a sociological enterprise not directed primarily towards the discourse and its knowers, but capable of providing a sociology *for* women. We might attempt to develop *for* women analyses, descriptions and understandings of their situations, of their everyday world and its determinations in the larger socioeconomic organization to which it is articulated. (1979, p. 172)

In this formulation, the typical qualities of feminist methodology— the emphasis on grounded subjects, on the investigation of everyday

life experiences, and the ways in which both material life and consciousness reflect the gender and class arrangements of the larger
society—are meant to serve *all* women, both knower and known. As
Mary O'Brien emphasizes, the transformation of individual consciousness in itself is inadequate. What is needed is the "transformation of
consciousness in the lived dialectics of people and nature." (1983,
p. 193)

While feminists share a commitment to attacking and ending gender
oppression, they are by no means unified in their analysis of the
underlying socioeconomic structures of society. This study is
grounded in the tradition of socialist feminism, and as such is concerned with the relationship of class, race, and gender. In this work,
I will employ the characteristic feminist methodology I have described
to investigate not only the effect of gender arrangements on women's
lives, but also the realities of class and race as well. Thus a focus on
women and the oppression of sexism should not blind us to other
forms of oppression. As Arnot comments, there is a "double division
of the world into antagonistic sexes and antagonistic classes." (Arnot,
1984) So in grounding ourselves and the objects of our research in
gender we must not lose sight of the complex web of power and
powerlessness resulting from our class and race positions as well. One
of the great weaknesses of liberal feminist research is that it ignores
other relationships of power than those based on gender. Too often
in studies of gender oppression, the effects of class and racial discrimination and the structural nature of racism and classism are ignored. Instead, women are treated as a single group, with no further
differences among themselves. But blindness to race and class leads
to as much distortion of social reality as does blindness to the importance of gender. A feminist theory that seeks social transformation
must take into account all forms of oppression and must actively resist
them.

The feminist methodology I have outlined can begin to show the
interrelationship of this "class/gender system." While the existence of
class cultures are sometimes denied in analyses of United States society, it is clear from studies of working class life that class position
is experienced not just in terms of control of material resources, but
is expressed within people's lived experience and personal relationships. (Komarovsky, 1967; Rubin, 1976; Sennett and Cobb, 1979) As
Rofel and Weston have pointed out, it is important to remember that
class is a *relationship* and that class interests will shift according to
one's work and access to various forms of power. (Rofel and Weston,
1984) Nonetheless, inherited class position is also extremely important,
as it provides various kinds of "cultural capital," and thus limits or

opens access to education and subsequent work. Thus it intersects with, in a material way, gender and race expectations and ideology. Class places limits on what is possible through access to material resources, but it is also experienced through ideology and as a subjective reality. Assumptions about our "right" to material comfort, education, and to have our needs met are deeply influenced by class as well as by gender-defined experiences. Attitudes toward individual achievement and collective needs differ for people according to their class location and class culture. While the relationship between gender and class is complex, a recognition of the reality of class is central to any analysis of the meaning of gender in social analysis. As Connell, et al. comment:

> Both class and gender are *historical* systems, riddled with tension and contradiction, and always subject to change. Indeed it may be better to think of them as *structuring processes* rather than "systems," that is, ways in which social life is constantly being organized (and ruptured and disorganized) through time. What is most important to grasp about them is their dynamics, the ways in which they exert pressures, produce reactions, intensify contradictions and generate change. (Connell, Aschenden, Kessler, and Dowsett, 1982, p. 180)

In the past few years, women of color have begun a critique of the feminist movement precisely because of its failure to address the oppression of racism in the lives of black women and other women of color and the meaning of whiteness for white women. (Moraga and Anzaldua 1981; Russell, 1983; hooks, 1984; Hull, Scott, and Smith, 1982) The essence of their critique is that white women fail to carry their own methodology beyond the limits of their own oppression. That is, white women too often argue that feminists must begin with their own subordinate position in relation to men, but fail to address the fact of their own dominant position as whites in relation to people of color. This failure to address their own power as well as their own subjugation leads once again to a distorted picture of social reality and fails to carry through a commitment to equality and full humanity for all women. Women of color experience an oppression of both gender and race and more often than not, of class as well. As Michelle Russell makes clear in her description of her work with poor black women, such women suffer a triple oppression in every moment of their material lives. We should keep in mind the advice Russell gives her students:

> In every way possible, take a materialistic approach to the issue of black women's structural place in America. Focus attention on the building where we are learning our history. Notice who's still scrubbing the floors. . . .

> Do we ever get to do more than clean up other people's messes, whether we are executive secretaries, social workers, police officers, or wives? Within what confines do we live and work? (Russell, 1983, p. 281)

If white feminists are to take feminist methodology seriously, and if we are truly committed to social transformation and the creation of a just society, we must be conscious both of the oppression of other women of color through racism, and our own position of power in a racist society.

I have spent some time in sketching out the importance of race and class in any critical feminist study of women's lives, because I want to make clear the underlying theoretical interests in this study. The methodology employed derives from the feminist research which has been developing in several disciplines over the past decade, but the theoretical interest in this study is much more clearly located in a more specifically socialist-feminist tradition, and one which takes seriously race and the realities of racism as inherent in contemporary capitalist society.

## SETTING

Any kind of qualitative research in public schools entails issues of confidentiality and protection for the subjects of research. Schools are highly political institutions, both in terms of their place in the community and in terms of power relationships among teachers and administrators in the schools themselves. Issues or conflicts that may seem only of academic interest to outsiders may raise deep antagonisms within the school community. Issues, for example, that I perceived as based on gender differences could also be and were viewed as conflicts between differing political or pedagogical views. The highly politicized nature of schools means that it is particularly important to protect the privacy and identity of teachers. At the same time, I felt it was vital to explore the kinds of conflicts and negotiations that are a part of teachers' experiences as women in traditionally male-defined institutions. Since power, both sexual and political, is an essential part of the social relationships in schools, I have felt it necessary at times to sketch out the tensions and conflicts that existed in these schools.

In order to disguise and protect the identities of these women I have not described in detail the sites in which they worked. This issue of protecting the identities of the subjects of research while remaining true to the actual context in which they move is always a difficult one. In this case, I have only generally described the two sites in which I did research. In these discussions I have tried to retain what is significant in terms of the structural constraints facing these women and the ways in which they are able to build counter-hegemonic practices.

Rather than provide individual biographies, I have organized this material around questions and general themes. But I have not created composite biographies, as Connell has done, for example, in his study of teachers. (Connell, 1985) In this analysis, I hope I have struck a balance between biographical studies and abstract analyses of teachers' lives.[2]

This study is not meant to be a classic school ethnography; it does not attempt to outline the full complexity of school social structure. Instead, it uses unstructured interviews and the analysis of classroom discourse to address the realities of these women's lives and to explore the themes that structure them. It is concerned with the ways in which teaching may be seen as counter-hegemonic work and with theoretical issues of resistance to oppression and class and gender reproduction. This work should be viewed as an exploration of issues; I hope it will raise questions and themes that can be pursued in further studies. Throughout, I deliberately employed the "conscious partiality" of feminist methodology in this research and made clear to the women I interviewed my own interest and commitment to feminist teaching.

At the outset, I do want to make some general comments about the sites in which I worked that I think are important to understanding the work of these feminist teachers and administrators. These two schools, like all public schools, feel the anxieties and pressures about education that exist in contemporary U.S. society. They are expected to provide a "proper" education for students, to teach them to read, to send the appropriate students to college, to provide others skills for working-class jobs; they are expected to teach students from other cultures English and to acculturate them into U.S. society. And the schools are expected to keep all the students off the streets and out of trouble. Given these overwhelming tasks, the remarkable thing about these schools is not that they fail in some of these tasks, or that they help to reproduce existing class structure, but that they succeed in so many cases in providing a humane experience for their students. This is the result of the work of a number of dedicated teachers and administrators who work in the face of cutbacks, social unrest and lack of understanding or support from the wider society. In my research, I was concerned with the feminist beliefs and interests of a group of women teachers, but they naturally shared the concerns and frustrations of all teachers working in public schools at this point in history. These concerns, which they shared with other teachers, men and women, were mediated by their feminist beliefs and their life experiences as women. But their teaching practice was shaped and deeply influenced by the structural constraints of the public schools in which they worked.

These schools were similar in many respects. Both were medium-sized high schools in a large urban area and both included a wide range of students in terms of class and ethnicity. However, they differed somewhat according to the class background of students. One site had a mixed working-class and middle-class population with a fairly large number of students from strongly ethnic and recent immigrant families. Urban schools increasingly must meet the needs of these kinds of students as the high level of immigration to the United States continues. This multicultural and multiethnic student population meant that teachers in this site needed to be particularly sensitive to conflicting class and ethnic as well as gender subjectivities. The second site was more consistently middle class and professional, although it, too, was integrated in terms of race and ethnicity. As we will see, feminist teaching and gender issues were affected by the different student populations in the classrooms of these two schools.

Both schools had extremely well respected administrators and both had women in high administrative positions. Both schools had implemented innovative programs and were open to political and socially concerned curriculum and courses from their teachers. This administrative attitude provided an unusually suppportive working environment for feminist and other progressive teachers. Both schools had participated at various times in experimental projects from local colleges, and some of the teachers had worked on collective projects with academic researchers. This collaboration gave many of these teachers the experience of participating in decision making in curriculum and pedagogy. In the case of the more middle-class school, an alternative school-within-a-school still existed as a very successful program, and was perceived by many middle-class parents as the most desirable program in this high school.

In both sites, the relatively close working relationship between feminist teachers and women administrators also provided these teachers a sense of and at least the possibility of community. They had experienced working situations (and some still worked in collaborative programs) which gave them a collective vision of what teaching could be like. They could share their work with colleagues and felt administrative support for their work. At the same time, tensions existed within both of these sites about questions of educational policy and curriculum. Both schools had complex histories of political and pedagogical struggles and staffs were still split about issues of educational policy and the role of teachers and schools. So while many innovative programs had been undertaken, there was opposition to both past and present programs within the teaching and administrative staffs of both schools. Faculty and administrators in both sites were categorized as liberal, conservative, and middle of the road by my informants. These differences in pedagogical and political views led to tensions and antagonisms, and in both sites feminist teachers felt themselves struggling against indifference and sometimes hostility on the part of other members of the school community. In both cases, the feminist teachers considered themselves part of a liberal (or radical, in some eyes) group of teachers who were more experimental and socially committed in their teaching. These kinds of struggles and conflicts around issues of educational policy were not unique to these two schools, but they do point out the ways in which schools are the site of contestation and struggle around a variety of very political issues.

Because of the financial cutbacks experienced by all the schools in this area and because of shrinking student populations, all of these teachers were roughly the same age. Younger, less experienced teachers had been fired, and new teachers were simply not being hired. These teachers ranged in age from 29 to 50, and the great majority were in their late thirties and early forties. Most of them had from ten to twenty years teaching experience and most of them had been deeply affected by the social movements of the 1960s. They had personally experienced social change and in several cases were continuing to participate in wider social movements. Again, this meant that their work was not isolated, but was experienced as part of a more collective social movement. This is not to say, of course, that these teachers did not share in the more general sense of political pessimism and sometimes despair felt in the early 1980s by many Americans committed to progressive change. Quite the contrary, these teachers were discouraged by lack of funding and misconceptions about teaching in the wider community, as well as a more general concern about the perceived shift in the political climate to more conservative and authoritarian values.

These feminist teachers were concerned with a variety of social issues, not just with feminist issues. But while other issues of race and class constantly emerged, the focus of my interviews with them was on their life experiences as women and on their roles as women teachers and administrators in this school setting. Because of my own interest in and commitment to feminism, I made clear to these women from the beginning that this study was focused on women teachers who were sympathetic to feminism, and their classroom practices or administrative roles. Not all of these women felt comfortable with the term feminism, but all of them felt a deep commitment to teaching as a means of bringing about social change; a belief in the dignity and equality of men and women was a part that commitment, as was a deep opposition to racism. As women committed to social justice and equality for both men and women, they were involved in attempts to transform accepted definitions of women's role and the common sense views of many of their students.

One of the key factors defining this group was that they were perceived by others in their schools as being feminists or as sympathetic to women's interests. They were identified to me in this way by one another. These women are in no manner meant to be a representative sample of women teachers in these schools, since each of them was suggested to me precisely because she was perceived as being sympathetic to feminism or social change. In my research, I focused on their teaching practice or on the administrative decisions that they made, and on their own life experiences and life histories. Ultimately, I worked with eleven women: seven teachers and four administrators. Some of these women I contacted through two key informants, women teachers I had known casually before I began my research. I met other women over coffee in the faculty room; others were suggested to me in conversations or formal interviews. I conducted several unstructured interviews with each of them and observed them in their classes and in interaction with their colleagues. Both interviews and classes were taped. I interviewed students, held group discussions with classes taught by feminist teachers, and used questionnaires to gain a sense of students' families and class of origin. Besides the formal taped interviews and classes, I spent at least one day a week for one school year in schools, either observing classes on a more informal basis or talking to teachers and students informally. When I had written up my findings, I discussed my interpretations with the women I had interviewed and tried to incorporate their own perspectives in my analysis.

Because of the methodology of conscious partiality used and because of my emphasis on the everyday lives of women teachers, this study can be placed within the framework of the feminist methodology I have outlined above. As such, I see it as a part of the emerging tradition of politically committed feminist research. This kind of qualitative research into individual lives rests on certain implicit intentions or goals. One of these is to provide an opportunity for the women who are the objects of study to discuss their work and to discuss the researcher's observations and analysis. The goal in this case is to provide an opportunity for reflection and a chance for dialogue about the nature of feminist teaching.

Another intention of this kind of feminist research is to reveal the valuable and committed work being accomplished by teachers. These feminist teachers provide a model of intellectual and critical work; in their lives they reveal the ways in which individuals are both shaped by history but also act to transform the future through their conscious struggle against what they see as oppressive in the past. High school teaching in general is exceptionally challenging and valuable work with exceptionally low status and little understanding from outsiders. A study of this kind counteracts the negative view of schools and teachers that is so commonly put forth. By revealing the struggles and achievements of feminist teachers in these sites, it can provide a model for the struggles of other feminist and critical teachers.

Finally, at a more theoretical level, this research contributes to the ongoing debate about the nature of schooling by presenting a study that acknowledges the forces of reproduction while exploring counterhegemonic and liberatory teaching. In this way it builds upon the critical studies discussed in the first two chapters. But it is also deeply influenced by the feminist methodology outlined in this chapter and can be seen as part of a larger feminist project. This feminist project shares many concerns with the critical educational theory discussed in the first chapter. Feminism calls into question existing definitions of reality to the point of questioning language itself. In the process it forces people to interrogate their own common sense view of the world and to move toward critical consciousness of their relationships and position in society. At the same time, feminism is committed to social transformation. Changing people's consciousness is not enough; real relationships and forms of power must be changed. As Freire points out, it is not enough for the oppressed to recognize their own oppression. That recognition is only the starting point for a movement to destroy that oppression and to become free in fact and not simply in the mind.

The ultimate justification for the argument that women must begin with ourselves and must begin to create a critical subjectivity is the recognition that changing the consciousness of women as subjects is central to combatting our oppression. As both Freire and Gramsci make clear, social transformation must go hand in hand with a critical understanding of people's relations to power and to production. Thus feminist subjectivity must be seen as a part of a larger social analysis leading to social transformation. As many feminists have pointed out, as women ground themselves in their own subjective experiences and question accepted definitions of gender in a fundamental way, they challenge men to recognize their own gendered position of power in relation to women and the ways in which their own thought reflects male hegemony through "male stream thought." (Black and Coward, 1981; de Beauvoir, 1961; duBois 1983; Mies, 1983; Rowbotham, 1973; Smith, 1979; Westcott, 1979) While this project is enormously difficult, not least because of the effects of racism, sexism, and classism that still permeate our consciousness, it is a project worth struggling for.

## NOTES

1. Stanley and Wise provide an example of a feminist methodology that is deeply influenced by ethnomethodology and interactive research. They critique feminist research that simply accepts a positivist paradigm or "adds on" women to existing male theory. They are critical of Marxist-feminist research which, they claim, simply subsumes gender to class. While they acknowledge the existence of what they call "dialectical marxism," they claim that "few signs of this are to be seen in the work of academic marxist-feminists, except perhaps in the work of Sheila Rowbotham." (1983, p. 45) But as I have argued in chapter two, a feminist educational theory is developing that takes seriously the dialectical tradition and attempts to address both structural forces and agency. In this chapter I have discussed what I see as a developing tradition of feminist methodology which is deeply opposed to positivism (in both its functionalist and structural Marxist guises) but which can be used to consider issues of critical consciousness and oppression in terms of gender, class, and race.

2. The question of teaching as work has been the focus of a number of recent studies which take gender as a significant area of analysis. Connell (1985) provides a valuable analysis of the data from the longer study undertaken by his group in Australia. Acker (1983) considers teaching as women's work; and Freedman, Jackson and Boles (1982) analyze the structural constraints that shape the lives of elementary school teachers.

**4**

# The Dialectics Of Gender In The Lives Of Women Teachers

*This ... brings us to the very heart of a fundamental problem that has always preoccupied philosophy—especially modern philosophy. I refer to the question of the relationship between subject and object, consciousness and reality, thought and being, theory and practice. Any attempt to deal with the relationship that is based on the subject-object dualism, while denying their dialectical unity, is unable to satisfactorily explain this relationship.*

*—Paulo Freire (1985)*

THE LIVES OF women high school teachers reveal the tension and dialectical relationship between "subject and object, consciousness and reality, thought and being" that Freire refers to. In their lives we can see the outline of the structural forces that have in some sense acted upon and created these women, but we also see their own growing and developing consciousness of the world they have inherited and their own choices and actions to change that world. The existence of this dialectical relationship throughout these women's lives is the major theme of this chapter. It can be seen in the early influences of family and schooling that led them to become teachers; in the impact of wider social movements and events that led them to become critical both of the society in which they found themselves (and in particular, the sexist ideology of male hegemony) and of the role society had defined for them. This growing consciousness has in turn led them to take certain actions both in their own lives and in their teaching to try to become actors in history who can in some measure transform the reality they have inherited.

Naturally their efforts toward change are uneven. As Gramsci points out, consciousness is "strangely composite" and always contains contradictions between hegemonic ideology and critical "good sense." (Gramsci, 1971) These contradictions may be brought to light, but they do not disappear. As Gramsci reminds us, hegemony is always being reimposed and human beings are always mediating and resisting the social forces that shape their lives. As Giroux comments:

> If we are to take human agency seriously, we must acknowledge the degree to which historical and objective forces leave their ideological imprint on the psyche itself. To do so is to lay the groundwork for a critical encounter between oneself and the dominant society, to acknowledge what this society has made of us and decide whether that is what we truly want to be. (1983, p. 149)

There is a constant struggle between people's capacity to think critically and the power of hegemonic ideology and the material constraints that act upon us. Life histories can reveal past struggles and oppression; they also show people in the process of generating self-critique as they struggle to understand the imprint of historical forces upon them and to act in the present in circumstances beyond their immediate control.

The debate about the relationship of structure and agency has found expression in critical educational theory in the opposition between theories of reproduction and those of resistance. As we saw in the first chapter, the fundamental problem facing critical educational theory is to understand the relationship between these forces, what Freire calls "the subject-object dualism." One of the goals of this kind of analysis is to approach the question of reproduction and resistance by examining the complexity of both forces within individual lives. This is in a sense similar to Althusser's call to "hold on to both ends of the chain" in social analysis. (Althusser, 1971) In this case, I think it means seeing the complexity of actions and individual consciousness within socially and historically defined circumstances. Thus actions are taken within existing structures, and a critical understanding of those structural forces, even a partial understanding (which is all most of us will ever have), can contribute to their transformation. Studying the complex lives and development of individual teachers counteracts the pessimism and mechanistic quality of reproduction studies of schooling and can reveal the possibilities and critical moments inherent in teaching. At the same time, the power of hegemonic ideology and the constraints of material life in a society marked by sexism, racism, and class privilege are delineated clearly in the stories of individual lives. The life experiences and choices made by these women reveal the power of ideology and of material forces on them and at the same time demonstrate their ability as human beings to understand, criticize, and act as agents in history.

In any analysis of individual lives in U.S. society, it is necessary to consider the power of various distinct but interrelated *social* forces. Gender, class, race, ethnicity, sexual preference, age, and physical ability all shape our lives. In this analysis, I have focused on the power of gender, class, and race. In each of these respects, the individual is forced to respond to a socially defined identity. In this sense individuals are not "free" to create themselves. They are born into and must work within existing social definitions of their own ascribed identity. And, as we can see, these constraints are both within consciousness (in Gramsci's sense of hegemonic definitions of reality) and in material restraints (only certain kinds of people will be hired for certain jobs; only certain people have the money to pay for the education of their children, etc.)

The kind of analysis which I have undertaken here attempts to unravel the ways in which structural forces shape the subjective experiences of individual subjects, while recognizing that it is on the terrain of everyday life that social relationships are reproduced and contested. This kind of inquiry is both complex and difficult to limit. As Dorothy Smith has pointed out, this kind of dialectical research does not require a sample of a population, but seeks to reveal social relationships in the accounts and experiences of subjects who live in the world. (Smith, 1986) But this also means that the life experiences of subjects begin a spiral of analysis that can seem unending. In this study, I began by focusing on women's lives and the meaning of gender in their life experiences. But it quickly became evident that it was necessary to recognize the importance of race and class as they intersected with gender in these lives. While I did not focus specifically on race and class when I began this project, the power and reality of these forces soon became clear in observations and interviews with teachers working in multiethnic and multicultural school settings. These forces were equally evident in discussions with these teachers about their life histories.

The class position of the parents of the women teachers in this study clearly affected their choices in terms of education and work. The parents of these teachers held jobs which would be classified as working class or middle class. One father was a professional (a minister); two were career army officers; two were small businessmen; four were factory workers or repairmen; one was an engineer; one was a truck driver. Only two of the mothers did not work at all; one had worked at a professional job before marriage; the others were secretaries or held clerical positions. Several had gone to work only after their children had gone to high school or left home. Only in the case of the businessmen and the minister was college a relatively automatic assumption on the part of parents. In the other cases, the girls either were encouraged by an older figure or had had outstanding academic success in high school and incorporated a general attitude from their classmates that "everyone goes to college."

The material determinants of class were relatively clear in the discussions about college choice, but equally important were assumptions about and the effects of racism. Evidence of the effects of racism on women of color is extensive. (Bunch and Pollack, 1983; hooks, 1984; Hull, Scott and Smith, 1982; Jordan, 1981; Moraga and Anzaldua, 1981; Walker, 1983) These writers emphasize that they define themselves as women of color and find it difficult to distinguish gender from race oppression; they are doubly oppressed. Each of the women of color in this group of teachers was profoundly affected by the existence of racism in U.S. society. One Asian woman, for example, who spent four years of her childhood in an internment camp during the Second World War, sees her scars of racism as more painful than those she has experienced because of sexism:

> I have a kind of double vision of this kind of thing. I see them as interrelated at least in my life and the life of other women of color. And that's another reason I don't go straight feminist.... Sometimes I go back and say well, I think racism is still a more important issue to me than feminism. So I kind of go back and forth on this. And a lot of times when I stop and think, well, if I was going to say which was worse in my life, blatant racism I think affected me more deeply than sexism. Of course sexism, I don't know, it's there but I think what really hurt me more emotionally was this thing about racism.[1]

Women of color felt that because of their race, teaching was one of the few jobs for which they would be considered. And because of their class, they did not have the resources to fight racist practices and beliefs through material privileges. The possibilities open to them were limited not only by lack of money (material restraints), sexism on the part of the wider society, their own internalized expectations of themselves, but racist practices and discrimination in hiring as well.

The white women I interviewed, on the other hand, while equally "raced," did not mention race as significant in their identity. That is, white women did not say, "Of course, I'm white, and that has deeply affected me." I would argue that this is precisely because as white they are in a position of dominance and thus do not identify themselves by race, since white privilege is so much a defined part of U.S. society that whites are not even conscious of their relationship of power and privilege. In U.S. society, white is the norm; people of color are defined as deviating from that norm and therefore their race becomes an issue. This is precisely what is meant by institutional racism. The failure of white women to articulate their whiteness is simply a measure of the way that all white people in this society benefit unconsciously from being in a dominant position.

In looking at these women's early lives the power of class, race, and gender in defining "common sense" reality and in limiting choices becomes clear. These themes of "being acted upon" by social structures and ideology are revealed in relationships within families, in early experiences of being a girl, in relationships with teachers and other adults, and in the difficulties individuals have in sorting out and becoming conscious of the power of material restraints and hegemonic ideology. The power of these forces is also revealed in later "choices" about careers and study. This is particularly obvious in the web of forces that led these women to give up other options (and sometimes, of course, they had no options) to become teachers.

## HOW ARE WE ACTED UPON IN HISTORY?

By examining the ways in which these women's lives are shaped and limited by existing social structures, particularly those concerned with gender, we are looking at the way girls are "reproduced" in a society dominated by male hegemony; more precisely, we can hear how adult women remember that process from their perspective at this point in history. What were the expectations these women came to have about themselves as they were growing up? How did they approach the central problems of their lives and what solutions did they develop? In powerful ways, both these problems and solutions were delineated by existing material forces and ideology. In looking at the way in which these women answered the question: What will I do with my life? we can see both material restraints and ideology acting in complex and reinforcing ways upon individuals. It is important in trying to recreate social "reality" from interviews to remember that the picture of the past is being reconstructed from memories, and that the memories of individuals are, of course, selective. But that does not mean that the mythical individual past cannot tell us a great deal. Through an analysis of these memories of why decisions were made, which structural forces had power, and what each person believed to be true, we can begin to see the power of history materially to shape human experience. (Johnson, 1984)

The interviews I conducted were primarily concerned with education and with educational choices, but the underlying themes of women's identities in this society also were touched upon. All of the teachers, in talking about their teaching, mentioned the value of nurturance and caring in themselves and their work—values that are emphasized as positive aspects of women's experience in this society. (Gilligan, 1980; Hochschild, 1975; Bowles and Dueli-Klein, 1983) But all of the teachers had difficulty isolating and remembering the specific incidents that shaped them as girls. When asked about how they acquired their gender identity ("What were the things that made you a 'girl'?") most respondents were unable to think of specific incidents. Their gender was so much a part of their identity that they were unable to distinguish the source of that identity. But the theme of nurturance and "being good" emerged from many of their stories. Here is one woman, who spoke of how she was treated as a little girl:

> I had a pink and white bedroom and I was really their little angel and grew up with a lot of that kind of not getting angry, not being particularly aggressive at all. I'm not sure if that was male/female or just their dynamics, or age or what ... I don't remember how that came to be. I think it's complicated. I remember just being labeled differently. Angel is the word that comes to my mind. To conform to that ....

This woman went on to say that her parents' expectations of her as a girl were subtle. She understood and met their expectations even though they were not overtly stated. As she said, "I think it was a lot more subtle, but just as powerful." Her memory is typical of many of the women in these interviews who do not identify specific incidents or statements from their parents or teachers, but recognize the subtle messages they were given. It is difficult to separate our present subjectivity from the historical forces that helped shape that subjectivity. But in this case, as in others, the expectation that a little girl would not get angry, would be a "little angel," surely indicates the intersection of social and familial forces in creating a woman's subjectivity. (See Belotti, 1975)

Others of the teachers were more critical of the societal and family expectations acting upon them. One woman, for example, grew up in the shadow of a very successful older brother who in her eyes was privileged in the family:

> He got to stay out late and I didn't and when I was at the age where he could stay out to a certain point, I couldn't because I was a girl. ... There's a lot of anger from me at him because no matter what I did—I was a better student than he was, he was brilliant but very erratic—but it wasn't as good as what he did because he was valued more because he was the boy. I was always spinning my wheels. So I would always do all these things to be better, and just have it discounted because I was a girl. Which just used to piss me off.

This woman recognized the inconsistency in the way she and her brother were treated and attempted to resist it, first by being very good, and then later, being "wild" as a teenager. This theme of feeling that families favored sons or had low expectations for girls is seen in this comment from another teacher.

> My father in particular never had very high expectations for the women in the family, for women, girls, didn't think that I should go to college, that I was obviously going to get married and that was going to be the end of it. Which is one of the reasons, I am sure, that at 45 I'm still not married. I was so damned determined not to fulfill that image . . . .

This woman was sent to public high school, but her younger brother was sent to a private boarding school, on to college, and has now taken over the father's business.

For one woman of color, her family's low expectations were a part of what she sees as the low status of women in her ethnic culture in general. She felt that both of her parents viewed themselves as failures because they did not have sons. But this woman also could not remember specific incidents of sexism when she was growing up:

> I don't know that anything was verbalized. She used to say, oh, I wish I had some boys, or something like that. But I can't really remember any incidents when she said things like that. Something tells me that somewhere along the way we heard that, or it was inferred in some way. I remember when my oldest sister had her first child it was a daughter. The second one was a son. And when she called my mother to tell her, it was a baby boy, she cried. And we thought that was very significant. Here she wasn't able to have a son . . . .

As girls, this woman and her three sisters were restricted in terms of freedom to explore and join in high school activities. This woman feels her mother's overprotectiveness influenced her sense of her own abilities.

> We felt she was very constricting and too overprotective in a lot of ways. Not letting us branch out and do a lot of things . . . I felt that it had a real impact on my development. I don't feel that I'm as risk taking as I wish I were. I wish I was more self-confident and adventuresome. And I think part of it is that she was so protective of us. It was easy to do, locking up four girls in the house. And we didn't go off on Saturday nights to the movies and things like that. I always kept saying, well if I were a boy I would have had more freedom. And I think I would have been treated very differently . . . .

While for some of the teachers, parental expectations were remembered as general or in terms of personality characteristics (don't be a risk taker, be a little angel, prepare for marriage and children, don't stay out late like your brother), for others these expectations were experienced as more direct limitations. They were discouraged from pursuing what they feel were real talents and interests. One woman, for example, was interested in science all her life, but was never encouraged to pursue her interest. Every Christmas she asked for a chemistry set, but never got one. At the same time, this woman's mother encouraged her to go to college and she was seen by her teachers as an exceptionally talented student. Other women were expected to help their mothers in the house while their brothers were free of these kinds of obligations; some felt their talents as athletes were not encouraged as were those of their brothers or male cousins. The effects of societal and family expectations on these girls is clearer when we look at their choices about college and careers.

All of the women I interviewed had some support for continuing on to college. In some cases (in more middle-class families) the support came from both family and school, but in three cases, the support came solely from their mothers, who were concerned that their daughters be able to support themselves (no matter what happened to their daughters' hypothetical husbands). One woman recalls conflict between her parents about whether she should go to college at all:

> It was the expectation of my father that girls don't go to school, college. My mother really had to fight with him and she really did battle with him to make sure that I got to college.... Part of the decision to go to [a small woman's college] had to do with the fact that I remember distinctly my mother saying to me, well, dear, in all likelihood you'll get married and raise a family. But in the event that something should happen to your husband it's very important that you have a career.

This theme of mothers who encourage their daughters to go on to college "in the event that something should happen to your husband" is echoed in other accounts. One woman recalls that her mother "definitely wanted me to go on to school. And took a lot of criticism from her friends. They even took a second mortgage on the house to pay for my first year at school..." Her father, who hadn't finished high school and was a mechanic, was not as concerned. Here is a similar conflict:

> My mother also, she encouraged me to go into business, to work for a corporation and she encouraged me to go to business college, which I'm glad I didn't do, because I'm not interested in business. But she did think of that. My father, I don't know what he thought. Everything I thought of, he would put down. I remember once I said I wanted to go to law school and he laughed at me. I was a very good student; I graduated Phi Beta Kappa ...

In other cases, both parents saw college as a kind of inheritance for their daughters as well as their sons. A woman of color remembers her parents:

> They wanted us to do very well in school. And study all the time and be industrious, don't waste time and don't spend money frivolously. And go to college. All four of us went to college. They didn't have the money to give us a big inheritance so they were going to make sure that we got a good education.

In other cases, these women were tracked in high school into college-bound academic programs and it became a group expectation that they should go on to college, even if it was not the expectation of their families or class of origin. Thus for some of these women, the meritocratic and formally gender-neutral nature of the public schools channeled them into college when their families, class, or the prevalent sexual ideology wouldn't have encouraged them. One of the women, for example, who was an outstanding student in both high school and college, and whose father was a factory worker, remembers a comparatively suppportive social environment in both her family and in high school; it was assumed that she would go on to college. But her experience was unusual, because of her family's encouragement of her to achieve whatever she wanted to in life. Unlike the other girls of the town, she was expected to go to college, and unlike most of the other women in this group of teachers, she was not expected to be a teacher or to "hedge her bets" in case her hypothetical husband couldn't support her. When she compared herself to other girls of a similar class background, the uniqueness of her own experience became clear:

> When in high school I was thinking about—what would I do? No one ever said to me, be a teacher, be a secretary, they said, be a doctor.... It was never expected that I wouldn't go to school. It was always expected that I would. So looking back, maybe I'm deducing some of this by comparison looking back on the way other girls were treated in the town. They were not all treated the same way. It was expected that probably they would not go to school and I think they were reinforced a lot for success in their social lives.

These women went on to college for various reasons and with different hopes and expectations. Some simply went on as a response to class or school expectations; others had more specific goals in mind. But of this group, only one women entered college with the clear expectation of becoming a teacher. All of the others had either no clear idea of their future or ambitions of other careers. By looking at the reasons for their decisions to go into teaching, once again we can see the power of societal forces and expectations of them as women and the power of sexism, racism, and the realities of class.

Several of these women had ambitions to become scientists when they began college. One thought of becoming a doctor, and considered majoring in physiology. Three other women wanted to become scientists: a geologist; a biologist; a chemist. But each decided to major in the humanities or social sciences, areas considered more suitable to women. And although each of them felt the decision was made by her and in her complete control, these decisions in fact show the influence of forces outside of their individual control.

In many respects, the most supportive school and family experience of all of these women was experienced by one of the women who later became a high-ranking administrator. Her father was a factory worker and her mother a secretary, and they had high hopes that their only child would gain an education and a profession. They hoped she would be a doctor. This woman was an outstanding student in her high school and when she graduated from her working-class high school, went to an elite woman's college and considered majoring in physiology. But once she was there, the realities of her class experience and earlier choices began to affect her. As she describes her early days at college:

> When I got there, I would have the experience of being the only person in the physiology class who had never dissected an animal or really done a laboratory right. . . . I didn't have any social rubric in my mind that allowed for educational and class differences, in fact. So I internalized it and said, they are smart and I'm not . . . .

This woman caught up with her classmates academically and soon did very well. But she did not continue in physiology:

> The fact of the matter is as I took more advanced chemistry courses I was a mathophobe, because I had not paid good attention to math in high school. I think I hadn't been taught it well, but I also think that . . . I have a block. I don't know now if that block is a real block, or if I have a learning disability, I honestly don't know . . . I know that if I have to pass a statistics course at the graduate level I can. But I really never took any math after high school so I realized that I would not be able to do graduate work in chemistry, which I would have to do as pre-med or whatever. I began to see that I had kind of closed that option . . . .

Here is another woman, from a more middle-class family, who also considered science, in her case, geology:

> Actually when I was in college I got off on certain kicks, too. Because the sciences became really interesting. But there were math issues that stopped me. I really loved geology and I loved the out of doors and I thought it was

great.... But in geology there's a lot of high math and that was something I didn't do. If you get into male/female issues, that's one of the classic ones.... I just didn't have the ability in math and didn't push for it. I pushed a little bit with a little science, and I enjoyed it, but nothing compared to some of my friends....

Another woman, who also came from a middle-class family, initially wanted to study biology; she changed her major not because of her perceived math weakness, but as she remembers it, because of a particular incident:

I was going to major in biology. I loved biology and I remember I had to stay one summer to take physics and I just had a terrible experience in the course and I vowed never to go and do that again. Because I really did love biology. I don't think this has anything to do with male/female, the teacher was sort of trying to weed out who had some previous knowledge and asked a very difficult question and said who didn't know. And I raised my hand and he called me to the board ... I had never heard of it and I felt so humiliated that I just said forget it. I don't know if that had anything to do with upbringing or not. 'Cause I could have just gotten angry and said, stay with it. But I didn't. I dropped out....

In each of these cases, the women made decisions because of what they saw as weaknesses in their academic backgrounds or because of an unwillingness to fight against these weaknesses. And of course their decision to change was immediately accepted as the correct one by everyone around them, and apparently by themselves at the time. Some women saw their talents in other areas. As they remember it, they made their choices rationally, because they were stronger in literature, history, or writing. Their fear of or weak background in math was seen as a reflection of their innate talents and not of a social pattern. Thus their choice to leave science was a "free" and individual one, in their own eyes.

When these women left science, they chose fields that led them into teaching. The woman who had felt humiliated in physics class reacted by turning to education: "Teaching just came because you had to make a decision and I remembered my mother saying that [teaching was a good career for a woman] and a lot of other women were going into it, it seemed to be a very female choice." The woman who left physiology decided to major in English, an area, as she put it, where she was "in the top one-half of one percent." When she graduated, she applied to two prestigious graduate schools, but failed to get into them.

This was my first encounter with real sexism, in that I had grades not quite as good as male friends, but I had grad record scores that were better. I had an experience where I applied to the same schools that a male friend of mine applied to. And he got in and I didn't. And I said, why is he getting in? At the time I attributed it to the fact that [her college] graded so hard, but why should they take a 21-year-old girl, when they could be pruning all these scholars, which is what they were doing. So a teacher said, why don't you apply to this [summer program], it's fabulous ... [At the summer program a professor] said to me right off, why do you want to go to graduate school? You should do what my wife does, teach in a junior college. First of all, he said, be realistic, they won't accept you. At least it was refreshing, someone finally said, straight out, they won't accept you because they accept very few women.

Needing a job to support herself, she took a job as a high school teacher.

Other women who studied the social sciences or humanities did so because of decisions made much earlier. A woman who eventually majored in English decided early on that she would avoid the sciences:

I did shy away from chemistry and physics. Not so much that I thought that as a girl I wouldn't do as well, I just felt personally, I was terrified to take either chemistry or physics. The only specific thing ... I loved art and I had an art teacher who was male. I was thinking at one point of going into commercial art, and he strongly discouraged me because he said it was a highly competitive, really vicious world and he thought even more so for a woman. And he was very clear about that.

It was clear to this woman that she had been influenced by her art teacher, but she could not identify the source of her "terror" of chemistry and physics, any more than the woman who could pass graduate-level statistics courses could explain why she was a "mathophobe." When this woman was an undergraduate she thought of going into social work, but her father, who had not wanted to send her to college in the first place, refused to pay for graduate school:

I had been thinking about going into social work, which meant going to graduate school, and my father said, look, if you really want that ... I will concede, I will pay for four years of college, but I will not pay for anything more than that. If you want it, you have to work for it. And I was either not committed enough or confident enough or whatever, so I said, all right, I'll do something else. I saw an opportunity to use some of the same skills in teaching, which has been borne out in terms of the focus that I have in my teaching, where I put my emphasis. So I went to the school of education.

The same recognition of decisions made, but uncertainty about *why* these decisions were made is expressed in other accounts. Here is a woman who majored in French in college, and who had dropped out of both math and science in high school:

I should have had some tutoring probably in math, because I know I'd done well in algebra I and in geometry, but I missed something in the beginning of the year and the rest was just C's and D's. I have no sense of that teacher really connecting with me to find out what was going on ... I did physical science. Nobody ever particularly encouraged me to take science. I did well with it, liked it, avoided it for the rest of my life. I don't know why. Nobody ever encouraged me. I have no understanding why ....

Her decision to become a teacher was made without too much questioning, as she remembers it. Somehow it seemed a "natural" thing for a woman:

By the time I was a senior I figured it would be teaching and I did the student teaching ... and I think that probably falling into a teaching position was just an extension of everything that women are supposed to be, which is nurturing and all the rest of it and that probably had something to do with my choice of going into teaching.

One of these women did want to go into science—chemistry. Like the others, she dropped science and, in her case, ended up in the social sciences. But her reasons for changing were not her perceived academic weaknesses, but because of a more immediate material situation. She was clear from an early age about her interests: this was the woman who always asked for a chemistry set for Christmas when she was growing up, but never got it, since it was an "inappropriate" gift for a girl. She also came from a working-class family and attended an elite woman's college. But after two years, she got married to her high school boyfriend. He was studying at another University, and so she transferred to be with him once they married:

I was majoring in chemistry, and wanted to be a research librarian. My first husband was studying business administration and he was going to be an accountant. When I switched ... I couldn't have finished at the same time he did. But I could have, if I'd switched into accounting, which was something that always interested me. But I can remember making the conscious decision not to switch into accounting, because he was majoring in accounting. And because there was no way I was going to compete ... I finally ended up majoring in [the social sciences] because that was as far away from business as you could get, plus it was something I liked and was good at. But I do remember that conscious decision, because it was an option for me. Because I always was good at math and I like that kind of thing.

In this woman's case, what influenced her was not her perception of academic weakness, but her acceptance that she should defer to her husband. He had a career mapped out; she transferred colleges and changed majors to fit into his plans. Her acceptance of a sexual ideology saying that he was the main actor in life and that she was subordinate to him led her to concrete decisions that she took "freely." But she also felt the effect of institutional sexism. She was unable to graduate with her husband because she had a baby and was not able to register on time:

> [The baby] was born on September 11. You supposedly had to be in school that following Monday. I did not quite make it. I made it a week from then and they would not let me take any courses at all. Absolutely none. That put me a semester behind. . . . So [the university] was a mixed experience.

This woman moved with her husband to the city where she now lives. She completed her degree in social science at the state university. Just before she went back for her senior year, her husband left her; she moved back in with her parents, and tried to find work that would support her and her young daughter:

> So I said, I've got to find something that I can do so I can support myself and I don't have the money for a master's degree. You've got a semester to go, why in heaven's name don't you get your [teaching credential], just in case. So that's what I did. But . . . when I finished I realized that teaching was ideal for me. I had the summers off, my daughter by this time was in first grade, I had the same hours she did. It provided a good salary . . . I didn't type, so therefore . . .

This story reveals clearly the effects of both a sexual ideology that tells women they should be subordinate to men and the material restraints and scarce resources of a working-class single mother.

The power of sexist practices to influence college and career choices can be seen in other women's stories as well. In particular, sexual exploitation and sexual harassment have enormous power to influence women's choices. One woman, for example, had gone on to do graduate work but dropped out of graduate school to become a high school teacher. Among other reasons, she left because of her discomfort with the sexual use of power in her department:

> I had done this master's program in [social science]. We had this department head who was just the worst. Talk about a radicalizing experience. This guy was such a pig, he was just the pits. He used to come on to the young women all the time. The department was just a sexual morass. Who's sleeping with who? I remember being nineteen and having this guy make a pass at me and thinking, what does he want with me? Like dumb. You never knew how he was dealing with you, whether he was coming on as a dirty old man or the head of the department. It was a real mix of sexuality and power. It was bad. Anyone who had any kind of quality got out of there.

This woman did not suffer "overt" sexual harassment, but the threat of sexual power made her deeply uncomfortable. While she now (and probably then) recognizes the corruption of power such a use of sexuality entailed, she was unable to oppose it openly. Instead, when a job teaching in high school appeared, she left graduate school and became a high school teacher.

The use and abuse of sexual power is even clearer in the case of another woman who had an affair with one of her professors. Because of her relationship with him, she changed her major so they wouldn't be in the same department. As she reflects on her experiences in college, she feels career decisions and her ability to take advantage of college were influenced and colored by her relationship with this older man:

> When I was in college I had an affair with one of my professors who was 28 years older than I and it was a terrible experience because I was 19. I've since read articles about this and books, you know, about girls in college having affairs with their professors. I think these professors, they leech onto their really good female students. To a boy student they'd be a mentor but to a girl student they're a lover.... The kids in his classes admired him, he was older and brilliant and had his Ph.D. from [a prestigious university] and I was this little girl, I was 19 years old and I'd hardly dated in high school. I was not precocious or promiscuous or anything. So I missed out on a lot in college because I was with this older man for years. It was kind of a secret....

This woman was very successful academically in college, but was uncertain what she wanted to do with her life. Finally, she did graduate work in education and became a teacher:

> I did get into law school but I didn't go because I was living with a man then and he wouldn't go with me, and I got into [a British university] and I didn't go, again because of a man. I was going to get a master's studying the nineteenth century British novel. So I did try to do other things, but I just didn't have enough confidence. I needed a woman mentor in my life, who was successful, who was a professional at that time, and I didn't have anybody.

This woman was in all formal respects a very successful student. She was accepted into prestigious graduate programs. But her feelings of being exploitated and always deferring to what seemed to her the more important careers of men led her to teaching, a career that seemed to allow her both to work and to meet the needs of the men in her life.

Three of the women chose teaching as a career while they were undergraduates. For them, the choice to become a teacher reflected what they saw as the realities of their class and race positions. One woman of color spoke of her need to get a job and her awareness of the difficulties she might face:

> I thought I wanted to major in history, but I ended up majoring in education because I knew I could get my credential and I knew I had two other sisters who had to go to college. So I thought, well, I'll do this and see if I can get a job. And I was lucky to get a job ... I knew I was going to be limited in terms of what kind of jobs I could get. I was quite aware of that. And even getting a teaching job was going to be difficult, because they weren't hiring a lot of minorities. You'd hear all these things about black people and [the city] wasn't hiring them and how difficult it was to get jobs ....

Only one of the women in this group had wanted to be a teacher from an early age. This woman decided she wanted to be a teacher while she was in high school and attended a city teachers' college:

> I took all the tests; I liked teaching. I spent my junior and senior year [of high school] tutoring kids in [a poor part of the city], that's how I spent my afternoons, a program run by the city, I applied and got the job. I always liked working with kids.

But this woman did not finish her degree at the teachers' college. Instead, she got married after two years, and moved with her husband to the suburbs and had children of her own. Eventually she finished her degree at the local branch of the state college while caring for her five children and participating in political movements:

> I would be standing at the stove with a book over here, a baby over here ... I did, that's how I spent my time. Yeah. It was very funny. So I went back to school and they were giving me a lot of hassle. I was the only older woman in the early 60s. I was a radical, I was well known in the whole area to be against the Vietnam war. They eventually found out that I was hiding Marines in my cellar, who had run away from Vietnam ....

For this woman, teaching was a natural way of expressing her already developed sense of social responsibility and activism. In many ways she had to struggle the hardest of all of these women to obtain a college degree, but at the same time, she felt in control of this choice and perhaps most confident about the value of her work as a teacher.

In considering the choices these women made in going to college and in becoming teachers, the power of material restraints in terms of sexism, racism, and class are illuminated. In many of these cases, women simply did not have the resources to make other choices— the money to pay for graduate work, for example. In other cases, the realities of sexism and racism meant they would not be considered for other programs or jobs. But equally important here is the power of ideology as these women "make sense" of the social world they inhabit. It is the internalization of a male hegemony that leads women to devalue their own worth and to assume that the career of a man is more important than their own, or that they are somehow "incapable" of doing math or science. Thus even when choices are freely made, they are choices made within a kind of logic of existing social structures and ideology. And this logic is learned very early and is reinforced through many institutions. Thus we see in these stories the valuing of female nurturance, and at the same time women's sense of inadequacy; an acceptance that men are the *real people* and that girls and women are there to support them. The hopes of these families for their daughters, the way paid work was presented to them, their assumed need to raise a family and to defer to their hypothetical husbands led them to see teaching as the ideal profession for a woman. Thus while these women made choices, they were at the same time profoundly "acted upon" through the ideology and material restraints of the social situation in which they found themselves.

## HOW ARE WE ACTORS IN HISTORY?

Throughout these accounts of growing up and making career choices, women recount decisions made and situations in which they felt they were acting "freely," but in which, as we have seen, social expectations and structural forces powerfully affected and limited the choices they made. And whatever their hopes and early plans, they found themselves teaching, doing work traditionally accepted as appropriate for women. Thus through their own choices, another generation of women teachers was reproduced. But in interviews they did not view themselves as passive creations of "fate" or social structures, but as individuals who had changed and who could have some influence over events in their own lives. They saw their teaching as important in encouraging students, often particularly girls, to take control over their own lives. They defined their own work as teachers as part of a struggle to create a more just society. In this way, they all in some sense defined themselves as agents of social change and resisted accepted definitions and the existing arrangement of society. Although they teach in public schools, which are defined by reproduction theorists in various accounts as "ideological state apparatuses" which reinforce and reproduce existing class (and gender and race) structures, they do *not* define their own work as part of that process. How can we explain what has happened to these women to lead them to question the social world they inherited and to attempt to change it?

I think it is important here to keep in mind that although human beings inherit a social world, they always maintain the possibility of what Gramsci called "good sense," by which he meant the ability to critique and understand what has happened in the past and what is happening in the present. People have the ability to create a utopian vision of what might happen in the future, of a different social world that might exist. This capacity for critique is reinforced and encouraged by certain historical conjunctures and personal experiences. In the case of these women teachers, their age and the historical events through which they lived are key to understanding what has happened to them and the ways in which they have changed. It is their own reflection upon what they have lived through and their ability to apply values and abstract ideals to their own experiences and life histories that has led them to change in their own lives and to assert the possibility of change in the lives of others.

First of all, these women have been profoundly influenced by wider political and social movements. The older of them lived through the civil rights movement, the resistance to the war in Vietnam, and the emergence of the women's movement. Some of them were attending college during the late 1960s and early 1970s and were influenced by student groups and movements; the younger of them were profoundly influenced by the growth of the women's movement and experiences in women's groups. For women of color, the civil rights and black power movements encouraged them in antiracist struggles. For white women, these movements led them to a consciousness of racism that has found expression in both their private lives and in their work as teachers.

Second, several of these teachers participated in various educational experiments in the 1970s. They helped establish some highly idealistic experimental programs in their schools, programs emphasizing social justice and participatory democracy. This group involvement in educational experiments founded on a belief in education as a means for social change deeply influenced these women's views of what teaching means and could become in a more just society.

Third, many of these women recount a strong sense of social justice in their lives from the time they were very young. As they grew up and lived through various social and political changes, they came to apply these abstract principles of justice to their own situations and their own lives. In particular, the growing consciousness of sexism and their oppression as women led them to see themselves as agents in history who, although they had been oppressed, had become conscious and thus in greater control over their own lives. This belief in their own ability to understand and to resist oppression in their personal lives then became the foundation of their own work as teachers. In looking at the particular expriences of these individual teachers, we can see these themes clearly expressed.

Many of these women first became involved in political and social movements while they were at college. The widespread social activism of the late 1960s and early 1970s provided them with a model of active commitment to social change that they brought with them to their work as teachers. Two of these women attended large state universities with active student movements in the late 1960s. While these women were not leaders of student movements, they were influenced by the events around them. As one woman remembers her decision to become a teacher (one made in part because her mother told her it would be a good job for a woman): "I started thinking that education could effect some change. And I participated in demonstrations, but I wasn't a screamer, or anything. But inside I would say definitely . . ." Another woman started her own alternative school immediately after she left graduate school in education. Here is another woman who began teaching with a vision of social change influenced by her experiences as a student:

> I think I came in with some kind of radical vision of really changing education. I think a lot of us had that back in the late sixties, early seventies. I had been active politically in college and I really thought that if you bought into the system in the sense of working for it, you could change it. And I think to some extent that's true.

Several of the women were influenced by participating in women's consciousness raising groups or by the emerging ideas of feminism as they affected other social movements. One politically active woman who has been involved with political movements "since the campaign of Henry Wallace," recounts her involvement with feminist ideas in the late 1960s:

> A lot of my friends were old time socialists. We couldn't believe that when the meeting times started we were the ones who were supposed to [make the coffee]. I mean it was a stupid, simple little thing like that—and then when the young college girls started coming into the group, and they would say, yes, SDS treats us the same way, then we said, well, we ought to get together and talk about it. We didn't know it was called consciousness raising, and it was at the time that I heard about the [local] feminist organization and [another feminist group] and I became involved with both of them . . . I had a consciousness raising group in [her town]. It was the late 1960s. My oldest daughter was in it too, she was a teenager. She was part of the same consciousness raising group. It sort of made sense to be a part of this whole thing. It made for a lot of conflict in a lot of ways with the anti-war movement. But I had read my history of the abolitionist move-

ment, too. I knew how women were used in the abolitionist movement and I realized that this is not anything that I want to be used as.

This woman was involved in the feminist movement from an early date, and was quick to see the connections between the ideas of women's rights and equality and her own life experiences.

Some of the younger women entered young adulthood when these ideas were more widespread and were affected by them at an earlier period of their own lives. Some joined consciousness raising groups immediately after graduating from college. Another woman was out of the country during the late 1960s; when she returned she felt initially alienated from feminist ideas and only joined a consciousness raising group later:

> I remember distinctly coming back to [the city], where I had been living before I left, and meeting a woman whom I hadn't seen obviously in couple of years and she said to me, you know there's a women's meeting going on and it's a consciousness raising group. Would you like to come? And I said to her, oh no, that's all right, thank you very much. Here I was, a world traveler, I had just spent a year and a half in Israel, Africa, India, Cambodia, and I had been traveling for the last six months alone, and I had negotiated countries, languages, so I felt so personally powerful that I really believed that I didn't need my consciousness raised at all, that my consciousness was as heightened as it possibly could be. It was years before I really understood what the women's movement was about. And years before I ever joined my first consciousness raising group. And discovered what that was and how unconscious I was.

Another woman also felt initially that the feminist movement had nothing to say to her, since she personally was clear about her own politics (in the anti-war movement) and her own personal identity. It was only later that she changed her mind about the need for a women's movement, because, as she said, "the journey is not an individual one, it should be a group one."

While all of these women were influenced by the ideas of feminism, the views and definitions of feminism they express are not uniform. They present a variety of perspectives about what feminism means as a movement and what it has meant in their own lives. Some women identify themselves easily as feminists. For one woman, being a feminist entails involving herself in political work on women's issues:

> For me a feminist is someone who not only believes that all people have the potential for achieving what they want to achieve but will struggle and work hard to see that it happens. When I look at an issue, I know that I'm a feminist because I define things in those terms ... I just don't believe anybody should have control over my destiny. Or my daughter's destiny

or your destiny or your daughter's destiny. I guess that's what I mean by feminism.

For this woman, her feminism is based on her own experience with discrimination as a woman, but also on her assertion that women as human beings should be free and should be treated justly. Thus her feminism is in a way an extension of her wider commitment to social justice. Here is another woman who also feels comfortable identifying herself as a feminist:

> I think I am a feminist and I think what that means is being very aware of myself as a woman, both politically and sexually and I think that I really am tuned into a lot of issues and a lot of people in terms of . . . how they impact on women. That's very broad and I guess that's where I think it belongs. All of the ways in which issues and attitudes impact on women. And because I feel very sensitive to those kinds of issues and feel very strongly that women need to be aware. I think that on that standpoint I would qualify as a feminist.

Another woman who considers herself a feminist says, "It means that I believe in equality for all people including women." For other women, feminism also entails the assertion that women should be able to do what they want to do. Some women make their commitment to women's issues very clear in their teaching. As one woman says:

> I think if you'd ask my students, they'd call me a female chauvinist. I find that with high school students you have to lay it on a little bit thicker than you ordinarily would. I feel very strongly about women being able to do what they want to do. I feel strongly particularly for high school students and I think this is one of the roles of women teachers (or men teachers, although they don't seem to do it very often). But for women teachers particularly to encourage female students to put their expectations as high as possible. . . . It's important to me that the women students . . . become aware of what it's like being a woman. In terms of the fact that there are still discriminatory practices against women and that I really have always believed, and I still do to a large extent, that women have to work harder to get whatever they want.

While some women felt comfortable with the term feminist, other teachers were uneasy with the idea of being labeled, particularly when they weren't completely sure they agreed with what the term feminist means. One woman, for example, while presenting a strong "feminist" viewpoint in her teaching, did not feel herself to be part of an organized movement. Instead she described herself "as a feminist, but sort of a grassroots feminist. Not a theoretical one." Another woman had difficulty with the idea of being labeled, but also with what she saw as the limitations of a feminism that failed to take account of race and class as well:

> When I think about feminism ... at the time that the movement first really became a movement, a lot of the things that were said did not attract me, although the wisdom and truth of a lot of what was said *did* attract me. But I did not identify with elements of it at the beginning that were quite middle class. That alienated me and so I never adopted that term for myself. As the movement matured and as I matured and as things were described more complexly, in ways that took into account minority populations and more and more class issues, then I felt very much identified with a lot of those issues and that women were doing a great service for all of society in bringing that issue out.

But while this woman felt sympathetic to certain ideas of feminism, she still did not feel comfortable with identifying herself with the label. For her, feminism could be defined in various ways, and she wasn't comfortable embracing all of those possible definitions:

> When I think about it in a positive way, it has to do with a definition that takes into account not only the well-being of women, but takes into account the well-being of society at large. That definition I like and as I hear more and more of that I feel helped by it and buoyed by it and more and more able to identify with it. It's funny, as you ask me that question, I find myself hedging. I have a lot of trouble with any kind of label. Partly because if people are going to apply that definition to me, are they going to apply the definition I like or the definition I have trouble with?

Other teachers had similar reservations about the term feminism. One woman, for example, felt uncomfortable with the term, even though, as she said, "it's rather odd" since she had done "a lot of feminist kinds of things." But she did not like being identified with what she saw as a "party line":

> I've always pulled back from the word. But then again I have trouble being parts of groups too. It's always a struggle for me that way, so I think of feminism as maybe more of like being organized ... it's like being a Democrat or something, you are a party member. So I always have a little trouble because then there's the buying in of hook, line, and buying a party line, possibly.

This dislike of labels is shared by others among these women. One woman who felt it was important that women "get in touch with the power that they have and recognizing it and being able to use it," still did not like labels. For her, "when you say feminist, it sounds pretty radical and I don't think I'd say that."

Other women would not identify themselves as feminists, but felt their commitment was to a wider concept of humanity. As one of them said about feminism:

> I'm not sure what it is. I think if it means that women should develop themselves as individuals instead of traditional roles and stereotypes and

just as people, then I'm all for it. And I've always kind of lived like that.... Just the fact that I'm sort of aware of that and struggle, makes me a feminist. But I'm not sure if that's what feminism is.

Although this woman felt uncomfortable with a formal definition of herself as a feminist, she had taught a women's issues course a few years earlier and came to see "that things I had always thought about were part of something bigger." One woman of color also had never defined herself as a feminist. For her, racism was probably a bigger issue in her life than was sexism. She defined feminism as

a kind of philosophy for women to be able to develop and act to their full potential. In a way, you can say, you can go beyond that to say, humanism is the same kind of thing.... Unfortunately our society's not at that place where we can look beyond this sex roles ... I think that's ideal, to see everyone as human beings. I look out and hope that's what will happen. We may not even be talking about feminism.

While these women's identification with feminism or involvement with organized groups varied, in every case they were influenced by the basic assertion of the feminist movement that women's lives and experiences have value. This took the form of a re-evaluation of their own lives and personal relationships and made them conscious of what they were doing as women teachers. Although as we have seen, they were all deeply influenced by male hegemony as they grew up and suffered to varying degrees from sexist practices in their youth and adult lives, they were able to critique those experiences and to act in their own teaching to influence their students to be conscious of sexism and to oppose it, even when they did not identify themselves as feminists.

These teachers were influenced not only by the changing political and social climate of ideas and wider political movements which gave them a kind of counter-vision which they could use to make sense of their own experience, but many of them were also deeply influenced by their participation in idealistic educational experiments. This direct experience of participation in these experiments often provided these women with a sense of their own power and possibilities as individuals working within a social setting. In other words, it was not just a change in consciousness made possible by a counter-hegemonic ideology (the civil rights movement, the anti-war movement, feminism), but direct personal involvement in attempts to change society that transformed their own definitions of themselves.

The schools in which these women work, like many other U.S. high schools, felt the effects of the widespread social questioning and demands for reform of the 1960s. In response, the schools established experimental and pilot programs, sometimes created by teachers and administrators internally within the schools, and sometimes created jointly by teachers and administrators working with professors and graduate students from local colleges. In a sense these programs were a kind of laboratory for educational experimentation. The presence of academic researchers with strong ideas of progress and the need for reform in the schools led to conflicts among the staffs of these schools; splits between "reformers" and "traditionalists" developed which still exist and which I will discuss further in the next chapter. The teachers I interviewed who were teaching during this period of experimentation were deeply involved with the reformers. This involvement deeply influenced them and their view of their own work.

These schools also felt the effects of the social unrest of the 1960s and 1970s. Both schools are racially mixed and tensions between blacks and whites sometimes erupted in school and became a focus for educational reformers. The fact that programs in the school were seen as actively addressing racism and social injustice had a profound effect on the teachers who participated in them. One teacher remembers this time:

> It wasn't that people were talking about issues of race or whatever, you were living these things day after day in a very intense way. You had to learn how to talk to this person, you had to work through difficult situations, somehow you had to get through a situation where there would be rioting outside the school and all over [the city] and you'd look out the window and here'd be the tactical police force and the dogs and the kids out on the street. And some stranger comes in and says, all you black kids shouldn't be here in this school with these white people. You should be over here in [the black area] or here or there or wherever. And here we were, the black and white people in the school, kind of making it together and being in this incredible conflict. I think you don't go through things like that at a formative time of your life, when you're 28, 29, 30 . . . you don't go through an experience like that and not be profoundly affected. Most people who've been involved with that project [an experimental program] will say that it had a profound influence on their practice and on their lives.

This woman is now a high ranking administrator and her direct experience with the experimental programs of the 1970s has had a great influence on her work. Because she has experienced a situation in which the status quo was questioned and conflict was directly addressed, she has a vision of possibilities for change that sustains her in the face of current difficulties.

These educational experiments affected other teachers as well. One of these programs was set up as a "school-within-a-school" to emphasize a respect for the individual student, and offer greater course choice and closer relationships between teachers and students. This program still exists; several of the women teachers I interviewed at this school taught at least one course in the program or had been involved with the program previously. The close relationships among the staff of this school-within-a-school and the sense that teachers there were collectively involved in a positive educational experience for their students was central in these teachers' view that their work "made a difference" in the lives of their students.

A similar program was set up in the other high school under the guidance of a professor at a local college in an attempt to create a program based on participatory democracy involving students, which would emphasize concepts of social justice and moral development. This program now only exists in a truncated form, as a kind of core program for a small group of students. But although the program is now greatly reduced, the intensity of the earlier experience has had a profound effect on the teachers who were involved in its formation. They still remain in contact with the other teachers who worked with them in the program. Here is one of these teachers:

> [That program] was a real intense shared experience. We met one night a week after school from seven to one in the morning every week. This went on for four years. This was with [a professor], with all the people from [the college]. So it's just an intense, very difficult, sort of having a vision of how you want schools to be, and even though that group of people are no longer in the program, they've moved on to other things.

Two of these teachers continue to work closely with one another in their teaching. Two other teachers meet one day a week after school to discuss their teaching. Their recognition of the need for mutual discussion and support, which is often disregarded in the structure of schools, is a result of their experiences in these collectively run educational experiments.

The effect of actively participating in collective movements is also clear in the case of the impact of feminism. Just as these women have been influenced by the ideas of the women's movement and partici-pation in consciousness raising groups outside of school, so they have been influenced by common experiences of sexism or feminism within the school. One woman remembers her experiences at the school-within-a-school:

> There was a much younger and very politically radical young woman who has since gone on to do labor organizing, in factories, who was part of the faculty [of the school-within-a-school]. And she used to raise questions all the time about it. You know, why were the women baking all the cookies

and typing all the agendas, and I really up to that point totally bought into that and suddenly I thought, yeah, my god, why are we doing this?

The next year a new head was appointed to the school, whom this woman describes as "a sexist pig."

> He used to run these numbers on us. He used to sort of strut around in pants that were too tight. The women by the middle of the year were just vicious about this guy. The young woman said to us, look we're not getting a fair shake. We're doing all the same work that the men are doing, and in addition we're baking the cookies and typing the agendas.... That was how it started. We got together once a week, all the women on the faculty, and we started talking. And that was the beginning. A whole world opened up that I had never been aware of. And that group continued for a couple of years and it changed in lots of ways. Our agendas changed, the leadership of the school changed, people got married, people got divorced, people had babies, people struggled about having babies. As the years went by new people came in and some of us had been there for a long time, but that was it, that was clearly the beginning for me.

This woman had been familiar with feminist ideas, and supported them. But she did not apply them to her own situation until she was in a group situation in which experiences and feelings were shared. And although she no longer belongs to a women's group, her view of her own life and her own teaching has been deeply influenced by this personal experience.

The youngest of this group of teachers is the advisor to the girls' group in a vocational education program. She attended college at a time when feminist ideas were more widespread, but did not participate herself in a woman's group. Instead, it was her experiences dealing directly with issues of sexism in the trades with her students that led her to reevaluate her ideas:

> You know, having worked with this girls' group a little bit, I guess I'm having my horizens broadened through some readings and through magazines and through talking with other women. Also ... I have a couple of friends who are more radical. So I've heard more of that over the last couple of years. So trying to weigh out what exactly is the situation, I have all this input ... I don't think the structure outside is very bending, and is very accommodating at all, but I think that there will definitely be changes simply because the women coming up are a lot stronger. I see it more and more in the kind of support that's being built, whether it's for wife beating, or children abused, whether it's rape counseling. An awful lot of women's issues are coming out of the closet and you hear more and more about that.

While this woman has been influenced by the reading she has done and the work she has done with the girls' group, in terms of peer support she has been very isolated. As one of only three women in the vocational program at this school, she has to provide support for the girls in the program virtually alone. She does not have the experience of working in a group to create programs or address problems collectively. This makes her work much more difficult; she looks to women outside the school for support for her work with the girls.

Each of these women teachers has been influenced by social movements and ideas which challenge hegemonic ideology. And as we have seen, participating in social experiments and movements and *experiencing* social change led these teachers to see that the status quo is not eternal. This ability to learn from and critique our own experience is at the base of the human ability to change and to act collectively to create social change. Thus these women reflect upon their own experiences; they are able to apply the lessons they have learned in collective social movements to their own personal lives. The effect of the ideals of self-determination and democracy of the civil rights movement on women has been well documented and is clear in these teachers' accounts. (Evans, 1980) The women's group that formed around issues of sexism at the school-within-a-school is another instance of women applying abstract ideals of justice and equality to their own situations.

This abstract sense of social justice and morality is a quality that exists in human beings, even when they do not analyze their own place in existing social structures or when they do not have adequate information about the nature of injustice or oppression. This innate sense of justice is referred to by some of these women as a part of their view of the social world from an early age. One woman, for example, whose parents were "not very liberal," seems always to have been sensitive to political issues:

> A teacher of mine has told me that I was liberal from the day she knew me. That I was always interested in what was going on in the world and had very definite ideas. My mother swears it was [the state university] that did it to me, ruined me politically for life ... I often wonder how I turned out the way I did, considering my upbringing. But my teacher said, she had me in sixth grade and all through high school, and she said, you didn't change. You were always the same.

Another very politically active woman also traces her political interests back to her childhood.

> As I say, in 'forty-eight I worked for Henry Wallace. I was also very active in trying to integrate the Campfire Girls while I was in high school. We used to go on hostels all the time and there were blacks and whites in our high school. And that wasn't tolerated and we got a lot of hassle over it.

> And that's how I became involved in antiracist causes. I hadn't really made the connection before, but I was always very sensitive to people's oppression, to people being oppressed.

This woman went on to be involved in the anti-war movement, in the movement for the rights of disabled people, the women's movement, and most recently, the nuclear education movement. It is her ability to apply these abstract ideals, which she has held from an early age, to changing circumstances in her personal life and in political and social causes that makes her an agent of change.

It is clear from these women's accounts of their early life that they have been deeply influenced by hegemonic ideology (particularly that of sexism) and by material structures. As women, they incorporated social and emotional expectations in their choices of career and in their personal lives. Women of working-class backgrounds faced the limitations of resources and inadequate education as well. And women of color faced the oppression of racism. In all of these ways, these women were profoundly shaped by the historical circumstances and social position they were born into. But as we have seen, they are also able to reflect upon their own experiences and to apply moral values to their own lives. What we see now are mature adults with rich and complex lives; their capacity to change is the result of the interaction between their critical consciousness and their place in history, or, as Freire calls it, the "dialetical unity" of subject and object.

While these women are critical and conscious actors in history, the institutions in which they work, large public high schools, are subject to material and ideological forces that may act counter to their goals or values. In the next chapters, I turn to the practice of these women in classrooms and in administration.

## NOTE

1. Quotations throughout are from interviews conducted between October, 1983 and June, 1984.

# 5

# The Struggle For A Critical Pedagogy

THE LIFE HISTORIES of women teachers reveal a dialectical relation-ship between structural forces and consciousness or agency. This dialectical relationship is also apparent in the goals of feminist and antiracist teachers and administrators and in the conflicts that arise as they attempt to put their beliefs about teaching and education into practice in urban high schools. Feminist and antiracist teachers and administrators hold certain beliefs about justice and equality that they try to put into effect in their work. But they inherit positions in already existing, highly complex institutions. In their attempts to put their beliefs into practice, the conflict between the power of the institutions and the critical consciousness of these women is highlighted. In their practice we see the conflict between their vision of what teaching and schooling *ought* to be, and the reality of working in a large bureaucratic institution. Feminist and antiracist teachers and administrators who seek to redefine curriculum and social relationships inside and out-side the classroom find themselves in conflict with existing patriarchal ideology and hierarchical relationships.

To try and capture the complexity of this situation, in this chapter I examine the goals of these women and the conflicts in and limitations on their practice that they meet in the school. This chapter explores the beliefs and practices of teachers as they attempt to create what I have called a feminist counter-hegemony. This is expressed in feminist teachers' articulation of what they feel is being attempted, what is achieved, and what makes success or failure possible. These goals naturally come into conflict with the structure of the school itself, and a conflict is set up between the institution and these teachers, whose values are opposed to the patriarchal and hierarchical structure of the school and who are in many ways seeking to oppose and change the institutions in which they work.

## WOMEN AS ADMINISTRATORS

Traditionally women have occupied subordinate positions in schools; they have been classroom teachers, while men have occupied positions of administrative power. (Strober and Tyack, 1980) The two sites in which I did research are unusual in having powerful administrative positions held by women with strong feminist and antiracist consciousness. The presence of women in these critical institutional positions provides support in both an ideological and a practical way for the feminist women teachers in these schools. One of the teachers commented, for example, that she feels the female dean of students is the "intellectual underpinning" of what is going on in her school. The position of these women administrators in the bureaucracy of schools provides them with certain opportunities to exercise power; at the same time, however, they are constrained in a variety of ways. They exercise power within the clearly understood rules and practices of a hierarchical structure; their position of authority influences and limits the solidarity and collectivity which they share with like-minded teachers, since they are institutionally not equals. They also meet resistance from teachers and administrators who disagree with them politically and ideologically. And of course, they are confronted with the criticisms of public education from school committees, parents, and media that everyone in public education faces at this time.

These women administrators all share certain similar goals in what they are trying to accomplish in their jobs. As administrators, they have the opportunity to articulate curriculum goals, to introduce new materials, and to encourage and support teachers in attaining those goals. Common to all of them is the desire to create a school in which all students are respected and in which the students' cultural heritages are acknowledged and valued. One of these administrators, for example, made the decision to stay in secondary education rather than continue graduate work in English. One powerful reason was her experience in an experimental program in the late 1960s and early 1970s:

> What I was learning about the range of people who could work together and be in school together and the power of being together in a setting, learning together, and engaging each other in dialogue and dialectic—the power of that to really, I don't want to say change society, it's too grandiose, but the power of that to be a major intervention in people's lives in terms

of how they thought about issues of race and sex equity and class issues and about education and their own hope for the future.... Now I think the dilemma is, is there any way to translate some of those things from a smaller setting where I can see that they work, to a larger, institutional setting, because the original notion back in '69, '70 was to make an intervention that would have some impact on public schools at large. So that's what I'm struggling with now: is it possible that these things can only happen in small settings, or is it possible that some of it can translate to larger settings? I don't know.

This woman's hope, then, is that schools can facilitate social change and the creation of a more just society. Her vision of schools is deeply influenced by the cooperative and democratic values of the experimental programs she participated in in the late 1960s. But as an administrator who must deal with issues affecting all the teachers and students of a large urban high school, those goals become much more difficult to achieve.

These women administrators are deeply committed to fighting sexism and racism and put their beliefs into practice in the kinds of materials they suggest, in hiring practices, in workshops, and in conferences. They see schools as important in bringing to consciousness racism, sexism, and classism but they also recognize the importance of respecting the cultural values of all students. Here is one woman administrator:

> I guess what I'm trying to do really is remove the barriers that separate people. Which I consider to be artificial. I think that we have to do that through the relationship that we have with people and through the curriculum that we choose to teach teachers or to teach kids.... Through curriculum and teacher training I'm trying to deal with all these little things that are in people's minds that they never even think about that are racist or sexist or class based or whatever.

This woman thus sees schools as places where ideology can be made conscious, and where prejudice and social stereotypes can be addressed in ways that challenge both students and teachers to reflect on their own beliefs, to articulate them, and perhaps to change them:

> I feel that anybody in any phase of education who doesn't ask kids to look at what their assumptions are about people or things, to look at their value systems, is not doing their job.... How do I know that I'm right? Is that going to change next year? How do I know that? But let's look at it.

While these women are sensitive to sexism and recognize their unique roles as women in positions of administrative power, they define their roles in much broader terms than simply a focus on women's oppression. Instead, they recognize the complexity of race, class, ethnic, and gender oppressions, and seek to create ways to raise issues of social oppression that will address their students' own experiences as black, Asian, hispanic and white; male and female; from working-class families, middle-class families, and families in poverty.

Raising the issue of women's oppression creates conflicts in multicultural and mixed class settings in which students often carry with them the patriarchal values of their families. These women administrators are all conscious of the complexity of these issues and the conflicts that can arise for students. One of them gives this example of the kinds of conflicts that can be raised when the school calls into question accepted behavior for girls in traditional ethnic or working-class families. Each year, students in a social studies class in this school go out into the city and interview elders for an oral history project. One year a girl from an immigrant family wanted to participate, but her father objected:

> Her father didn't want her to be involved in it. He ... only wanted her to come to school, come home and help with the family.... It was a very patriarchal family. The father had an iron fist and he ruled and everybody listened to him. In the interviewing process, we had to sneak this girl out into the community to interview these women. In the process she got the notion that she wanted to go to college. That caused such tension in her life that it was horrible. [We] felt so guilty, we felt so awful about this kid who was going through all of this. But she did go away to college and she's going into her junior year of college next year.

In this case, the school opened up ways of thinking and acting that were unacceptable in the culture of the girl's family, but, while the administrator felt guilty about the conflicts that were being raised, she still encouraged the girl to participate and explore different ways of looking at the world. This brings up again the ways in which the values and vision of teachers may conflict with the family and cultural values of students. This administrator argues that teachers and the schools must be sensitive and conscious of these kinds of conflicts:

> While I don't like to set kids up against their parents, I still realize that in a sense our children are not our children, and that they really have to make a life for themselves in this world. How much is the responsibility of the school? I don't know. It's very hard having a 14-year-old Portuguese kid in the school who's an adult at home, and in Cape Verde would be out working and not in school, and helping the family. We keep the kid in school until 16 and encourage him to stay longer and go to college. We need as much cross-cultural work as we can possibly get. Otherwise we can be an affront to these people.

Key to this argument is the idea that children in schools are not the "possession" of their families, but that they must be challenged to expand their own self-consciousness and to become critical of both themselves and the world in which they find themselves. But at the same time that she argues this, this administrator continues to insist that teachers must be sensitive to the importance of each student's family, class, and cultural values.

Some of these women administrators themselves came from ethnic working-class families. Working in urban high schools, they are sensitive to the conflicts of gender, race, and class that emerge in the classroom. Black women administrators are particularly sensitive to the need to celebrate cultural diversity and to assert the value of the language and culture of all groups in U.S. society. They are sensitive to institutional racism and to the need to combat an ideology that says mainstream white language and culture is the norm against which all other groups should be measured. One white woman of working-class background argues that it is necessary "to integrate visions and views of women's roles with visions and views of class and culture." She argues that a teacher should raise questions that acknowledge the validity of what students are experiencing:

> It would seem to me that a teacher should be able to introduce a topic such as, how do you think your life is going to be compared to the life of your mother's generation? What do you think it's going to be like to [ethnic] women of your generation? Do you think your life is going to be pretty much the same as your mother's or do you think it's going to be different? In what ways? What would be the advantages of some of this? The disadvantages? Do you think that the way that you are now is threatening to your family at home? Why? To me that would be a much more open, spacious conversation than saying, women should do this . . . There must be a way of elucidating in a way that encourages people to take a more dynamic view and to see possibilities for themselves that are different from what happened to their own family, or maybe even are going to be the same, but to feel all right about them.

This woman is thus arguing that conflicts should be recognized and addressed in the classroom. She also emphasizes the need to see students not as the "possession" of their families, but as historically and socially situated individuals who experience conflicts. The key to working with these complex issues lies in the sensitivity of individual teachers, who must be supported and encouraged institutionally. For these women, this is one of their major roles as administrators.

These administrators attempt to achieve their goals through various methods. As administrators, they can bring ideas to the attention of teachers, hire (but given the tenure situation at these schools they rarely can fire) teachers, and encourage the kind of curriculum and discussion they hope to introduce. But the teachers are the ones present in the classroom, and the power of administrators to bring into being the kind of teaching and learning they desire is limited by the beliefs and practices of these classroom teachers. One administrator, responsible for overseeing curriculum for an entire high school, encourages certain trends and curricula through meeting with the coordinators for each of the disciplines in the school:

> I tried to introduce that as an issue of goal setting with all of the coordinators and I tried to help the school develop a definition of multicultural education. I think we should address the content of curriculum and the context in which disciplines are presented. We also need to look at staffing patterns since teachers are role models. Does the staffing pattern reflect the student body? In other words, students should find something about their own sex identity and their own racial and cultural identity in the content of the subject, particularly in areas [such as] social studies and language arts, but also in other areas like mathematics and science.

This high ranking administrator works closely with departments over curriculum issues. She uses the example of a meeting she held with the humanities department. She explained the meaning of Title IX to the teachers of the department and pointed out to them that they could be held liable for sex discrimination in their classrooms. She remembers bringing in boxes of materials by women writers to the meeting:

> I'm looking at the curriculum and there is really very little by women writers and there is very little by minority writers and we can do better than this. Having somebody say, well, what books are there that are any good by women? And saying, well, I just happen to have some ... with this enormous box and having people walk by and say, hmmmm, well, I'll take this and I'll take that. So little things like that and sponsoring people to go to workshops and giving workshops myself...

In other departments this administrator encourages the department heads to look at course selection patterns in terms of both race and gender:

> I can go out and say, why is it that so many boys are taking this and so many girls that? Or I can make enough of a fuss so that a department head notices that there are two courses which are basically the same content, but one is described as fast and one described as slow and one has mostly black kids and one has mostly white. So he came to me and said, you know, maybe there is something to this, what should we do? So we said, all right, let's just give a test and see if there really is a difference. And all the kids come out basically the same which means that they have self-selected. In other words, there's a kind of consciousness raising that has gone on in the world about some of these issues that I think makes us more sensitive in ways that do affect people's lives.

In these ways, administrators hope to expand the limits of discourse about the curriculum. By making previously taken for granted behaviors and practices problematic, they encourage other teachers and administrators to consider ways that goals might be redefined and practices changed.

All the women administrators I interviewed are committed to a multicultural curriculum which values the gender, race, and culture of all of the students in these schools. This commitment leads them to challenge traditional curriculum and institutional structures within schools. They hold workshops for teachers in departments and attempt to introduce and encourage work on women's and minority issues. Some of them are active not only in encouraging teachers in their classroom teaching, but also work to connect the curriculum to political and social movements outside the school. One of the administrators organized a nuclear awareness conference attended by students from a number of other high schools; she brought in a group of elders from the community to speak with students about growing up in the city and about the problems of elders in the present; she encourages classes to examine the social problems of various groups in the city. In all of these ways, she both supports classroom teachers and introduces them to various social issues that can be addressed in their teaching.

It is not always possible for the goals of these women administrators to be met. These schools, like most U.S. high schools, have traditionally been led by male administrators. Many departments are overwhelmingly male. Many of these male teachers and administrators are not sympathetic to the antisexist stance and critical goals of these women administrators. The tensions between feminist, liberal women and more traditional and conservative men teachers and administrators varies among schools and among departments. Often this is not just a tension between men and women, but reflects wider differences of educational philosophy and political struggles within schools. One teacher describes her department, headed by a strong feminist woman:

> I just lament that there isn't a better working relationship in general within the ... department. It stinks. There are lots of reasons.... [One] issue is that [this part of the city] is so political that the people who grew up here and went to this high school and who are now teaching in it, really everybody else is an *Auslander*. We're outsiders and foreigners. And we're very suspect and we're seen, many of us, particularly the whole crew I just identified as liberals, maybe even major liberals, and there's a lot of resentment, a lot of animosity.... Sometimes it's people not even talking to each other, walking by each other and basically treating each other like

they were invisible. Sometimes it's in such overt behavior as, a suggestion would come up in a department meeting to do some work together or to put in some extra time and people will suck their teeth and roll their eyes. And there will be these great heavy sighs or these long exchanges of icy stares ...

The hostility or lack of response on the part of other teachers and administrators (male and female) can be deeply frustrating to feminist women and makes even more important the support they receive from one another. But while women administrators face frustrations and failures in their work, they also recognize their own value and achievements. While some teachers may oppose these administrators' educational philosophies and resist changing their teaching content or practice, those teachers who are sympathetic with the feminist and antiracist stance of these administrators recognize the importance of their support.

For women teachers, in particular, the fact that women with a sense of solidarity with other women teachers hold these key positions is affirming and provides both ideological and material support. For example, in one school the woman dean of students was mentioned by virtually everyone I interviewed as a person they respected and looked to for support. One woman teacher spoke of the importance of women administrators in this school:

I think this school ... from what I can see out there, there are some strides being made. I'm thinking particularly about those terrific women in positions of power in this school that I think have made a real difference. ... They're more supportive, they're more open to new ideas, they're caring about upgrading the quality of the classroom, they're certainly concerned about issues of race and sex in the classroom.

In another school, a woman teacher talked about the support she felt from a feminist department head in a largely male department:

[The department head's] been good, I think. She's been supportive and she's also a feminist. It's nice having a woman as a boss, that was really nice. In the department there are only three women, two now, because one's on maternity leave, and roughly 23, 24 guys. One of my friends said once that the usual social studies department is the athletic department writ small ...

Another teacher commented on the strengths of this department head and some of the difficulties she faces:

I think [the department head] is real good at bridging differences. There's something about the force of her personality that I think, I think the meetings are partly the way they are because of her. She's good, and easy, very supportive to me. I enjoy working with her. But I think it must be frustrating for her, because she's always trying to sort of, I think, get people to do things, and people are courteous and they give things a shot, but I don't know how much they're taking in.

For this department head, who has clear goals about creating a feminist and antiracist curriculum, the resistance of some teachers to changing their traditional teaching practice is deeply frustrating, but she maintains an optimism and belief in the human ability to learn and change, even in the face of these resistances and struggles:

> If you're in a profession, it's constantly changing and you are constantly in a process of self-improvement if you're a professional. A lot of people don't do that, they're not reflective. I can't imagine being a teacher and not thinking about what you do. That's frustrating to me.... In spite of conversations I have with them, stuff I've given them to read, workshops that I've done with them, some teachers are still doing pretty much the same stuff they were doing years ago. I'm one of those people who believes in people. I believe if you are supportive of people, and you help them in appropriate ways, that in fact they will change and do what they do better, etc.

This woman, like other women administrators I interviewed, must draw on her own deeply held political beliefs and her belief in the possibility of personal growth and social change to sustain her in a working situation in which she meets resistance from teachers as well as the frustrations of inadequate funding, pressure to cut staff and increase class size, and the political pressures on the school from the community at large.

These women administrators provided strong leadership for the teachers in their departments, both men and women, and worked hard to maintain good working relationships while encouraging teachers to expand their teaching and to consider new kinds of curriculum and materials. They were talented administrators and successful in their jobs. But they experienced frustration in what they could accomplish and some anger at the discrimination they had themselves experienced as women. Here is another woman administrator:

> I'm also a person who's very angry. I think that I'm very angry because I've spent a great deal of time working against being denied access. That makes you angry, and I am. I'm angry about a whole lot of stuff.... I really do have good leadership qualities. I know how to get people, I know how to stroke people and get the best out of them. And how to do a whole lot of things that help people be good at what they're doing. If I weren't a woman I would probably be some very high up school person or businessperson. And I just didn't have those opportunities. I've made a lot of my own opportunities and I haven't let that stand in my way. But I know my life would have been very different ....

Despite the difficulties they face, these women administrators all feel a sense of accomplishment at what they have achieved and a confidence in their own abilities. One of them, for example, although very conscious of the obstacles facing women in gaining positions of power and exercising that power, also makes clear her confidence in her own abilities:

> The more I think about it, the more I realize that I have not let myself be imbued with the notion of failure or not moving ahead or not being in a position of power because I'm a woman. I've not let myself think that way. Even though there have been things to struggle with and I'm sure that I would have done, I would probably be in a very different position now if I weren't a woman. But I think that I have always seen myself as someone who can do certain things, whether it's have power over people or help them change or whatever. And I think that for a woman my age, in her fifties, that's not a common trait.

Women administrators recognize the obstacles they have to overcome as women and have a strong sense of the value of their work as women in positions of authority. For black women in positions of power, their struggle has been to overcome not only sexism but racism as well. Black administrators recognized the difficulties they had overcome and the difficulties they still faced as black administrators in a white-dominated institution, but they also had a strong sense of their importance as role models for black teachers and black students. They were sensitive to what it meant for black students to be sent to an administrator and to walk into an office and see a black woman in a position of power and authority. As powerful and competent administrators, they also challenged racist assumptions among white staff and white students. While black women administrators experienced the isolation other blacks have described in being among the few blacks in a largely white administration, they also expressed pride and a recognition of the value of their work.

These women administrators also looked to one another for support. In each of these schools women administrators shared friendships and relied on one another for support in their jobs. One women described the importance of these networks of support:

> I've always managed wherever I've worked, to have women friends who are in similar situations to mine, who will share. I got a group together when I first came here ... there were about six of us and about once a month we used to go out to supper. And we used to share our frustrations. That was really nice, and then after [one of the women] left we stopped going out to supper, but we still can talk ...

Another woman administrator sees positive changes in the school over the past few years and recognizes her own role in achieving those changes:

I do think the institution has changed and I do feel good about that. And I feel I've had a part of it. In fact sometimes I think that I'm some of the major force behind it, I think that a lot of my thinking and my vision and my ways of talking about the school have been pretty important in making it happen. I hope a lot of other people feel the same way, I don't mean about me, I mean about themselves, and I think they do . . .

These women administrators' visions of what schools could be like in addressing issues of class, race, and gender provides strong leadership in the schools. They support innovative counseling programs, work to make other administrators conscious of race and gender issues, and provide support for teachers who want to introduce new curriculum.

All of these women administrators share a belief that they are competent; all have had some success in encouraging changes that will make these schools places where all students are respected and heard. That view of their importance and success is shared by feminist teachers in the school. The presence of women or minorities in positions of power changes the consciousness of everyone in a school, whether the presence of these people in these positions is welcomed, accepted, or resisted. At the same time, though, it is important to recognize and not ignore the limits of institutional change in public high schools. These limits exist not only in the resistance and political conflicts between administrators and teachers, but also in the hierarchical structure of the bureaucracy of the schools.

Within the institutional structure of the school and within existing parameters of gender, race, and class, individual administrators are profoundly limited in the kind of changes they can effect. When the relationship of administrator and teacher is defined as one of giving and taking suggestions (or orders) from the top down, individual teachers will resist. But that resistance can be subtle and difficult to address. Teachers are alone in their classrooms, and the discourse they encourage cannot be monitored or imposed, except in a demand for certain quantitative results. Teachers' attitudes and the value they place upon forms of cultural knowledge cannot be dictated by the administrator. Only a more open and collective form of discourse and power structure could begin to confront or change some of these practices. But because of the *apparent* power of the administrators, when change does not occur as they would like, they feel responsible, angry, and frustrated.

Administrators like these women are isolated by the hierarchical nature of the school bureaucracy. They may hold democratic and collective beliefs, but they occupy positions in a rigid hierarchy in which decision making and power is formally not shared. They have access to knowledge and forms of power not accessible to the teachers in their departments, and this structural role necessarily isolates them from teachers. In order to perform their duties in the jobs they hold, they may feel the need to assert their administrative role and the barrier that divides them from their staff. And that barrier may divide them from people who would be their natural allies.

By taking positions in an existing hierarchical bureaucracy, women administrators like these face structural limitations that create conflicts between their goals and the possibility of achieving them. And of course, they also face pressures from the larger society to achieve quantifiable results, improve reading scores, lower drop-out rates, which provide little support for their vision of school as a means of building a more democratic and just society. The ideals of social justice and a common good which underlay the experiments of the 1960s and early 1970s are absent from the present debate about schools. And it is in the climate of the present debate with its emphasis on order, control, and results, that these administrators have to work. So one question that the work of these administrators raises is, How much can an individual of good will accomplish in relative isolation and in the absence of larger movements for social change?

This question brings us back again to the question of agency and structure. While an examination of the work of these women administrators reveals the structural forces that shape and limit their work, it also reveals their importance in encouraging the work of feminist and antiracist teachers in classrooms. The presence of these women in powerful positions in the school is itself a message. While the goals of these women are profoundly limited by a hierarchical institutional structure, their commitment to struggling against sexism and racism provides support for feminist teachers in the school and is significant in making further changes possible.

Administrators attempt to influence what goes on in school by encouraging certain kinds of curricula, by introducing certain viewpoints and topics, and by calling into question accepted "truths" about students, knowledge, and teaching. However, they are limited by their position in an hierarchical institution and by the fact that they are not in the actual classroom in interaction with students. Classroom teachers, on the other hand, are more in "control" of knowledge and relationships in the classroom. Of course, this control is in many ways illusory. Teachers' actions are bounded by the same structural pressures and limitations that administrators face. In many respects, they are *more* limited, since they are also under the authority of the administrators. But in their choice of what to teach and *how* to teach, feminist teachers have the opportunity to call commonsense assumptions into question and to attempt to create more humane and to some limited extent, more democratic classroom relationships. Meaning is created in classrooms by both teachers and students, and by calling attitudes and deeply held beliefs into question and by valuing certain kinds of knowledge (the cultural knowledge of the students themselves, for example) the feminist teacher shapes and influences the kind of meaning that is created in the classroom.

## GOALS OF FEMINIST TEACHERS

Feminist teachers are articulate and reflective about their goals in teaching. Their goals and teaching practice reveal a commitment both to critique and analysis—both of texts and social relationships—and to a political commitment to building a more just society. As women who are conscious of sexism, issues of gender and sexism are naturally important to them as they reflect upon their goals in teaching. But for many of them, feminist goals become human goals; "human" in their discussions is often used interchangably with "humane," implying care and concern for their students as human beings. This sense of valuing humanity is expressed in their own sense of themselves as examples. As one woman teacher says, she sees herself as a model for students in "just a little humaneness and care." Another teacher speaks of her own relationships with students as providing an example of humane relationships:

> I think that kind of trying to make the school a more humane place and giving kids a place to be where they're comfortable and also to be able to relate to a teacher as a human being and not just an authority figure, I think that's the main thing.

This commitment to human values gives these teachers a sense of their own worth and the value of their work, even in a society where it is often devalued. While "humanity" may be a vague term, the meaning it is given here is one of recognizing the value of others (in this case students) and of one's self. One teacher calls this concern for others "somewhat a missionary zeal:"

> I feel so confident that I can help a kid, that's very important to me. The long term impact, I think you don't usually see, although I do have contact with some kids over the years, people who are not ten years out of high school, we get together and talk and share ideas. Some of it's just knowing that I'm raising a lot of these kinds of issues to kids. I do have somewhat a missionary zeal about humanizing kids or giving them permission, creating an environment in which they can feel it's okay to be human.

The goals of these feminist teachers include the creation of a classroom where "it's okay to be human" in terms of relationships, but they also include a commitment to raising issues and questioning accepted social values and ideology. This entails the encouragement of a critical interrogation of the media and the messages of the school itself. One woman defines her goal in teaching students about the ideological messages they receive:

> To sensitize them to be really cynical about what they read, what's given to them in any kind of context, whether it's the movies or reading.... I've asked this question, where are the others? The others can be not only women, they can be minorities. Is this accurate? What's going on here? And to teach them to be really sensitive to the whole idea of the hidden curriculum, ... the institutions that perpetuate that kind of sexism, racism, however you want to look at it, to really look for that.

Another teacher defines this goal as leading the kids to look at the world differently. She recognizes the difficulty of evaluating her success at this, since she is not looking for a quantifiable difference, but for a change of consciousness:

> I think that's difficult. It's like painting a house. When you finish you know it's painted and you know you've done something. We have no way of knowing. My major goal would be that at the end of the year ... that kids would look at the world differently. And that ability to look at the world differently would last. I can't think of any greater satisfaction than meeting a student that I had ten to twenty years ago who would still remember the class he took, but remember it because of talking, discussion, ideas.

Another woman calls this process of questioning accepted views of social reality "consciousness raising," and by this she means raising students' consciousness not just about gender issues, but about issues of race and racism as well. Like others of the teachers, she is concerned about the students' own commonsense consciousness:

> I think it's consciousness raising. I just want them to be aware ... I don't know that I will necessarily change kids' values, whatever they come to me with from their families. But if I can just make them a little bit more open minded. Or if I can make them aware so that they can pick up on things themselves, they can see where something might be a sexist or racist comment. It really has to do with raising consciousness. I would really love to think that some of them might through these conversations and things that we're reading, change some of their stereotypical patterns.

These teachers do not see teaching in terms of quantifiable results, test scores, or mastery of "facts." Instead, they are describing the classroom as a place where consciousness is interrogated, where meanings are questioned, and means of analysis and criticism of the social world as well as of a text or assignment are encouraged. For these teachers, the goal of teaching is grounded in a respect for the human value and cultural worlds of their students, and what is encouraged is the development of both criticism and self-criticism. As one of them says, "it's almost more a process thing than a content thing ... to try and make high school a more fair place, to try to empower kids in their lives not to be victims." For these teachers, the kind of power schooling can develop is the power of consciousness and critique. This calling into question of accepted versions of social reality may not occur in other areas of adolescents' lives, but for these teachers the classroom can provide the site of criticism, discussion, and intellectual struggle.

Feminist teachers share a commitment to a more just society for everyone, but they also have a particular sense of themselves as women teachers and are conscious of their actions as role models for students. They define themselves as gendered subjects and are conscious that their actions in the classroom have particular meanings precisely *because* they are women. This consciousness makes them consider both the content of their teaching and their own actions and appearance. One woman, for example, who works with vocational education students, sees her actions as having meaning for both boys and girls:

> I had this conversation in here with [a boy student] ... who said that women can't lift heavy things. So I picked up the mop bucket that he didn't want to empty and as I'm emptying it I'm saying, oh yeah? I talked about working at UPS, carrying packages there. And I think that since he's seen women doing these things that he will never again say that women can't lift that ....

Another teacher speaks of her actions in the classroom in a similar way:

> I certainly make a big deal about not being helpless in any way. I do my own macho thing. I'm sure I really go overboard in some ways too. I installed my own pencil sharpener, which meant getting hammers and nails and all of that, which I'm very comfortable doing, but I ... really made sure the kids knew that I had done it, that I didn't just turn it over to the janitor. Or when there's no window open in the room and the kids want windows open, I sometimes say, okay you open that one, I'll open this one and I'll climb up on the window sill no matter what I'm wearing, because I just don't wear clothes that don't allow me to climb up on window sills or run or whatever. I do feel it's my responsibility.

For both of these women, their actions have meaning precisely because they are performed by them as women. They want students to understand the message of independence and competence that they try to communicate by manipulating the physical world in a way that women stereotypically are unable to do. This is what one teacher implies by her comment that she feels it's her responsibility. As a woman teacher she becomes a symbol of what being a woman can mean, since as a teacher she is a public figure for students in the classroom.

This same sense of being a symbol or model for possibilities or potential ways of being in the world as a woman is expressed by other teachers. One woman, who was viewed by other teachers as quite a radical teacher, recently married and had a baby. She had taught in a junior high school before coming to the high school and felt that her pregnancy was important to students who had known her for several years:

> I think even having gotten married and pregnant was a powerful impact on a lot of the kids. A lot of the kids who had known me before, and went up to this high school and had seen me at the high school, they were real curious about why I decided to get married. . . . And it was the most positive thing for so many kids that I was pregnant. Especially kids that had known me a long time. It's very life affirming. . . . The nature of my work has always made me vulnerable to getting a lot of backlash or the whiplash. So when I did something like getting pregnant it was like, you're kidding! Because they'd always affiliated me as a commie pinko anarchist whatever, because I taught that kind of stuff and for me to do what in their mind was this happy, traditionally, female thing. . . . it was really terrific for a lot of them to see that those things can be together.

In a sense, this woman is reversing the message of female competence here. In her view, the students see her as a radical and a feminist, but they have a limited and stereotyped vision of what feminism and radicalism mean. Thus by getting married and having a baby while retaining her values in the eyes of the students, she challenges their accepted view of what is possible for a woman and presents an alternative future for them.

These teachers are conscious of students' stereotyped views of women teachers and consider ways of challenging those views. In one teacher's analysis, students often fail to respect women teachers because of sexism, because women are not valued in the wider society:

> I'm concerned that I deserve kids' respect, that I'm not dismissed as just another woman. Because I think that too often kids have experiences in schools—I'm not so sure it's true any more, but it's an old stereotype—kids not respecting their women teachers as much as the men, and a lot of that has to do with fear, issues of being afraid of men.

This teacher is also conscious of what she wears and of being fair to both boys and girls. But at the same time, she asserts her own knowledge and perspective as a woman and raises women's issues in her teaching:

I'm very concerned about on a very elementary level, with what I wear. I try to vary what I'm wearing, so I'll wear pants and I'll wear skirts, so that kids will see that it's all acceptable, you don't have to be one way or the other way. . . . I'm not seen to be favoring males or females in class, to really treat students with the same degree of respect. Whenever I have an oppportunity to point out women's issues or a woman's perspective as different from a man, or to do what I think of as correcting some misconceptions, I jump right in. . . . I'm quick to point out to kids that in terms of the dominant institutions in the United States, they have traditionally been controlled by white middle-class males. I key into those issues very quickly.

Another teacher repeats these themes of being conscious that she is a role model of what is possible for a woman and as a teacher:

I think it's important as a role model, particularly, obviously for girls, but I think it's important for people. I see myself as being some sort of free spirit and I think it's important for kids to see that, that you can be a teacher and not be a boring person. That's been sort of my mission—to be a role model, to break stereotypes and let kids know that as a teacher you can still have an interesting life . . . .

This teacher also is committed to raising feminist issues, a commitment that emerges from her own experiences:

I think it's a personal thing. It's almost like your own personal crusade. I guess that being of an age, someone who came up in the midst of the women's movement and when I look back at my own socialization and my own kind of intellectual training, I realize that so much of it was missing because no one ever thought of teaching it then. And to be sort of sure that's not going to happen again. So I think a lot of it comes out of personal experience, that kind of, a revelation if you will, when it dawned on me, in my early twenties . . . this has all been wrong.

Other teachers mention the same theme of raising feminist issues as something they personally feel committed to because of the sexism they have experienced in their own upbringing and education. One teacher comments:

I really do try to encourage the girls to do whatever they want to do. I talk about feminism and literature or writing. In the basic comp class I'll try to pull out articles that talk about those kinds of issues. Changing roles of men and women. And I also do that with racial groups and class, different classes. . . . Those are my values and also I want it to be easier for other girls than it was for me . . .

In their teaching, feminist teachers choose to address women's issues in a variety of areas of the curriculum—in the texts they choose to teach, in the topics they emphasize, and in the examples they provide. This is true both in courses that are structured to address women's experiences and issues and those of a more neutral character. One English teacher raises these issues in her discussion of language itself:

> I address the issue even when I teach grammar, for example, "everybody should do 'his' own thing," to try to get around that by using the plural. You know, our language is sexist and racist, and no one ever said that when I was in school. . . . I talk about feminism and pull out articles that talk about those kinds of issues, changing roles of men and women. And I also do that with racial groups and class, different classes.

One feminist U.S. history teacher adds women's and minority issues at the end of each section, since she has to work against the textbook:

> I try to spend at least a day or two days at the end of every era, going over women and minority issues, because their textbook doesn't. If you talk about the frontier, you talk about the effect on women, not just about the railroad tracks. If you talk about early industry, you talk about the Lowell girls. It's just a matter, if you have the knowledge, you can stick it in there. I try not to make a separate issue of it, it's just constant.

Few of these teachers felt they addressed issues or relationships in a typically "feminine" style. When they did, they were ambivalent about the message that such a style conveys. One woman at first could not think of particular goals she held as a woman teacher, but then considered her caring and nurturing style:

> The more I think of it, little things come to mind, I think my god, are those real stereotypical? Because the thing that came to mind was, I think there's a certain way I teach because I am a woman and was socialized and raised a certain way that they might not get from a male teacher, such as an emphasis on listening or emotional expression, or sensitivity . . . which is not to say I think men are not, but it may be a certain way of expressing it, may be more female, which I think is good for them.

This woman accepts a traditional role for a woman, that of sensitivity and openness to emotion, but asserts it as a positive approach. At the same time, she is uneasy that she is fulfilling students' stereotypes about women's identity and sphere. While she doesn't speak of consciously dressing in certain ways or consciously raising certain women's issues in her teaching, she is self-conscious about the ways in which her own ways of interacting with students may confirm their existing stereotypes. But in asserting that the "more female" way of expressing and defining issues is good for students, she validates women's experiences and approach. This raises the issue of how to assert the value of what are defined as typically women's qualities—such as compassion and sensitivity—without limiting the definition of "woman" to something innate and given. In other words, this teacher raises the issue of how we can recognize that gender is socially constructed while still valuing and recognizing the power of the way women do experience the world in this society.

Feminist teachers have their own agenda in addressing sexist practices and assumptions because of their own gender interests. But teaching in urban high schools, they also have to become conscious of the race and class identities of their students; the subject matter they teach is "read" according to the class, race, and gender subjectivities of their students and this different reading or knowing creates conflicts, which must be faced by the feminist teacher. These conflicts are particularly clear in cases in which the culture of the students conflict with the culture of the feminist teacher in terms of definitions of gender. In strongly ethnic families, either second-generation families with strong ethnic identities or immigrants, the accepted roles of men and women are often in opposition to the feminist beliefs of feminist teachers. This conflict can be a source of great frustration to feminist teachers and a source of doubting and questioning their own goals. One teacher speaks of her realization of some of these conflicts:

> There are very strong stereotypical roles for men and women in [this immigrant] community, for example, that's one of the places I see it most strenuously. Sometimes it's socioeconomic class. There still are a majority of working-class boys who feel that they have to head the household, they have to have certain kinds of jobs, treat women in certain ways, and there are still to my way of thinking sadly too many working-class girls who still accept that. I have to be very careful when I'm talking about kids' aspirations and attitudes to make allowance for those kids so that I don't either make them feel discounted or wrong. I really work on how I phrase things to try and give everybody space; in the meantime I'm working to get them to expand the limits of their thinking.

In this passage, this teacher touches on several of the problems for feminist teachers in their relationship with students from working-class and strongly ethnic families. She sees patriarchal social relationships as oppressive to girls and women. But at the same time, she respects the cultural and class identities of her students; in Freire's terms, she recognizes them as subjects who must be engaged in dialogue. Rather than condemn the arrangement of gender in her students' families, she, as she puts it, tries "to expand the limits of their thinking."

Balancing gender, ethnic, and class subjectives while remaining true to their own values and social/political beliefs is both difficult and can be frustrating. As one woman put it:

> When I first realized the degree to which I was going to have to compromise I was very angry and felt discouraged, but what I finally came to see was

> that I had to acknowledge what kind of culture these students were coming
> from. And it was really myopic of me to assume that what I was doing was
> so reasonable that any kid, no matter what kind of orientation he or she
> had had, would be willing to buy into it. That's really being almost an
> American ethnocentric. It's really not acknowledging the cultures and the
> home lives of these kids. So now I don't feel quite so defeated, I feel that
> I really have to get a reading from the group and figure out where they are
> and just try to work with them at that level. And open them up a little.

It is difficult to challenge the accepted values of students, particularly
when those values are a part of the dominant ideology. Feminist teachers place themselves in the position of bringing contradictions and
tensions to light in their teaching. This kind of critical teaching within
dominant institutions can be isolating and frustrating. Thus the presence of sympathetic administrators is highly important to these teachers. Equally important is the support they find from one another in
their working lives.

This solidarity and mutual support can be seen in the ongoing
relationships of teachers who have worked together in nontraditional
experimental programs over a long period of time. Collective decision
making and discussion of curriculum and pedagogy are built into
these programs. Teachers who have experienced this kind of working
situation try to recreate it in their teaching in other settings as well.
For one of these teachers, working collectively with other teachers
makes her work possible:

> I enjoy very strong working relationships with colleagues, so I do as much
> as I can to build that into my day or week or schedule. If I were just
> teaching in isolation with my kids, which is the way a lot of people prefer
> it, I think I'd die. . . . So I teach this humanities course in part because it
> means that I have a social studies teacher to talk with, I do [an experimental
> interdisciplinary program] principally because I'm really committed to the
> concept. But also because it means that I'm in daily contact with another
> teacher. And my Wednesdays, I work every Wednesday with [another
> woman teacher] and we arranged it so that we're both teaching the same
> curriculum in our ... courses. We meet right here at 2:30 and we stick
> around until 5:00, sometimes we talk about what we're going to do, some-
> times we write things up for each other, sit and correct papers together.

This teacher makes her job a more collective one by seeking out
programs in the school that require joint planning and discussion,
but she and another teacher also set up an informal meeting once a
week to talk about their teaching and to provide mutual support.

Other women felt more isolated in their own department and looked
to other women in the school for support and friendship. Here is one
woman's description of her relationships with other women teachers:

> I have a couple of friends who are teachers here— neither in [my department], but who are similar to me in perspective. I guess that's why we're friends— [a woman] who's in science and [another woman] who's in English and of course [the woman department head]. I don't see [another feminist woman in her department] as much. And she and I are very different in styles, which makes it difficult.

Although women in a department may have different teaching styles, they do share the common experience of being among the only women in a department and face similar experiences of sexist attitudes from their colleagues. They thus provide support for one another when these attitudes surface. One woman recalls an incident in a department meeting:

> [Another woman] and I were sitting there the last meeting and there was [a male teacher sitting behind me]. [Two other women teachers] and I were the only females. We were talking about . . . black women in history. It had been in the newspaper. Did you know? I said to [one of the women], That could be for your course and she said, Yeah. And the man said, What are you talking about? So we told him. And he said, Oh, that's just another example of women trying to make up history for themselves. [The other woman] just looked at him and said, "Back to your hole."

This incident is an example of the continuing sexism among the male teachers, but it also shows the importance of feminist women supporting each other. While all of these women consider themselves to be assertive and self-confident, each alone might have been less willing to confront the male teacher without the other sitting next to her.

The difficulty for individual women in responding to sexism can be seen in another woman's account of her reaction to sexist remarks by a male administrator:

> I have a lot of trouble dealing with some of the men teachers in this building who are so sexist it is excruciating. And I don't handle it very well. As recently as three days ago I went to an administrator and asked him to sign a paper for me to go to a conference on the teaching of women in literature. He picked up this piece of paper and said, Hey, I'm not going to sign this. And I knew he was kind of teasing, but it's the kind of teasing that I just find difficult to respond to. And I looked at him and said, uh, Okay. And he said, Ah, what can you do, how can you spend a day talking about this stuff? He said, There hasn't been enough that's been written that more than can fill this sheet of paper. It's that kind of stuff that I just, I want to lift my knee. I can't think of anything to say to that, it's such an ignorant response.

Unlike the two women teachers in the department meeting, this teacher did not challenge the administrator's remarks directly. But she was dealing with him alone and did not have the support of another woman. Instead, she was confirmed in her resentment and sense that she faces hostility and lack of support from this administrator. As this teacher commented, this incident was complex; because of previous encounters with hostile or uncomprehending male administrators, she was unwilling to engage what she saw as a "no win" situation. But it is also an example of the difficulty of responding to sexism in a situation in which the woman teacher is unsupported and alone.

The continued existence of sexism among the male staff in these schools makes the presence of feminist women administrators extremely significant for feminist teachers like these. But equally important is their sense of personal solidarity and support for one another in their daily working lives. By asserting feminist values, they oppose the patriarchal culture of male teachers and administrators, and find the support to raise feminist issues in their classrooms. Without this shared vision and values on the part of both feminist teachers and administrators, they would find it very difficult to try to expand and challenge patriarchal ideology in their teaching.

## CONCLUSION

The issue of teachers' work has been addressed recently in the work of several researchers and critics. The so called "failure of the schools" has been the focus of a spate of reports and national commissions. Teachers have been blamed individually for unimaginative and superficial teaching, for the high drop out rate of certain groups of students, for the perceived failures of the schools to turn out happy and *employed* students. Schools have been called upon to increase the quantity of requirements and to introduce competency tests for both teachers and students. Underlying these critiques of schools is an ideological view of both knowledge and students that assumes that knowledge is quantifiable and students are the passive recipients of that knowledge. The role of teachers then becomes that of the dispenser of knowledge. As we have seen, the vision of these feminist teachers and administrators is deeply opposed to this view of learning and teaching. Instead, they emphasize that students are knowers and the creators of knowledge. For them, the classroom is potentially a site where consciousness and ideology can be interrogated, where critical thinking is encouraged, and where for both students and teachers, "it's okay to be human."

Feminist teachers and administrators face difficulties as they try to put their ideals into practice, but these difficulties are the result of structural and institutional forces beyond the scope of their individual lives. Rather than focus on the supposed failings of *individuals* working in the schools, it is much more useful to consider the institutional structure of the schools as the cause of dissatisfaction or perceived "failure." Working from this perspective, critics have pointed to the increasing bureaucratic control of teaching; the demand for results expressed in increased testing and demand for quantifiable results; and the "deskilling" of teachers through the use of packaged curricula. (Apple 1982a; Apple 1982b; Cohen, 1985; Freedman, 1985; Popkewitz, 1982) In these analyses, teaching is viewed in the context of larger social forces.

One of the most significant and useful analyses of the effect of the instituional structure of the schools on the work of teachers is to be found in the work of Freedman, Jackson, and Boles in their two year study of elementary school teachers. (Freedman, Jackson, and Boles, 1982) They document the isolation of classroom teachers, their frustration at lack of control over resources, and the demands for quantifiable results on the part of principals and parents. At the same time, they note that teachers are deeply affected by ideological constructs and explanations for their feelings about their work. The use of the concepts of "burnout" and "deadwood" provides an ideological explanation for teachers' feelings of anger and frustration. Both of these concepts blame the individual teacher for her feelings of inadequacy. Through the use of these terms, teachers' feelings of frustration are interpreted as the result of their own inadequacy—either they are "burned out," that is, used up and no longer able to muster the energy and enthusiasm necessary to be a good teacher, or they are "deadwood," going through the motions of teaching, but no longer effective. The burnouts leave teaching; the deadwood remains but is inefficient. In both cases, the individual is at fault, not the institution.

Freedman, Jackson, and Boles argue that the truth is just the reverse. It is the institutional structure of the school with its increased managerial and bureaucratic control over teaching and its demands on teachers to transform children and to solve all their social and personal problems by attaining certain test results that creates a difficult work situation for teachers. As they argue:

> Teachers must now begin to turn the investigation of schools away from scapegoating individual teachers, students, parents and administrators toward a system-wide approach. Teachers must recognize how the structure of schools controls their work and deeply affects their relationships with their fellow teachers, their students, and their students' families. (Freedman, Jackson, and Boles, 1982, p. 132)

Thus Freedman, Jackson, and Boles deny the view that teachers' difficulties are the result of some subjective failure on the part of individual teachers or that the sense of failure and futility which has been called "burnout" is the inevitable result of teaching. Instead they point out the logic of the power structure of schools and the contradictory and conflicting demands made upon teachers by the wider society and by the very structure of schools themselves.

The high school teachers and administrators I have discussed here work within hierarchical and patriarchal institutions and, as we have seen, the parameters of their practice are set by the structure of those institutions. Schools are not isolated institutions, but reflect the logic and tensions of U.S. society as a whole. Thus the problems of inadequate resources faced by teachers and administrators and the ideological debates over the nature of teaching and the political role of schooling are a part of larger political and ideological struggles. But as we have seen, these struggles do not completely determine the practice of teachers and administrators. Individuals in positions of administrative authority are important in encouraging and supporting critical teaching; teachers do attempt to put into practice a vision of the classroom that is deeply humane and critical. While both administrators and teachers are bound by institutional constraints, they do have room to negotiate and create change. In this struggle between their consciousness and desire for social transformation and the power of existing social institutions, we see again the dialectic between agency and structure and the importance of mutual support and a critical understanding of teaching practice for individuals attempting to work politically within schools.

The power of dominant structures is expressed not only in the institutional structure of the school, but is brought into the classroom itself in the consciousness and lived histories of students. In the next chapter I turn to the conflicts of power and meaning in classrooms. By examining discourse in actual classrooms, we can examine what feminist teachers attempt to do in their classroom practice, and to what extent they succeed.

# 6

# Gender, Race, And Class In The Feminist Classroom

FEMINIST TEACHERS CHALLENGE sexist assumptions and call into question accepted definitions of gender. In their teaching, they attempt to counter the ways schools have traditionally reproduced patriarchal social relationships. They challenge sexist notions of appropriate behavior and work for women and men and thus come into conflict with the sexual ideology of the school as well as that of the larger society. But in challenging these assumptions, they also come into conflict with their own students, who themselves are embedded in socially and historically created relationships and who in many cases have incorporated into their own consciousness what Arnot has called male hegemony. (Arnot, 1982) Students, like teachers, are historically situated beings, whose complex subjectivities are socially defined and at the same time are internalized and lived. Both students and teachers have experienced and participated in relationships of domination, submission, oppression, and privilege which have helped to shape who they are and how they interpret the world. This recognition of students and teachers as historically situated subjects with conflicting gender, race, and class interests is vital to understanding the possibilities and limits of the classroom.

If feminist teaching is to contribute to what Giroux and others have called the building of counter-hegemony, then we must be conscious of the realities of various forms of oppression and the realities of intersecting and conflicting forms of power. (Giroux, 1983; Simon, 1983; Lather, 1984) As Giroux comments:

> The complex and dialectical nature of ideology must be stressed in order to understand human agents as multi-layered subjects; that is, as human

> beings who are more than merely class subjects, who exist as complex agents, who live in different "nows," who embody a number of historically formed subjectivities, and who are both formed by and act out of a variety of ideologies and cultural experiences. (Giroux, 1984, p. 129)

In order to grasp the possibilities of feminist teaching in mixed-class, multicultural classrooms, we need to recognize the complexity of these competing ideologies and histories. By seeing the ways that individuals are "multi-layered subjects" we can begin to unravel the complex interrelationship of teachers and students as they negotiate and mediate meaning in the classroom. As Gramsci reminds us:

> The starting-point of critical elaboration is the consciousness of what one really is, and in "knowing thyself" as a product of the historical process to date which has deposited in you an infinity of traces, without leaving an inventory. (Gramsci, 1971, p. 326)

The concept of "multi-layered subjects" points to the sometimes contradictory nature of this "infinity of traces:" that the power of gender, class, or race may be employed to counter oppression suffered through another aspect of our being. These are the contradictions and tensions between overlapping forms of oppression and forms of power that face feminist teachers in multicultural public school classrooms.

The need to recognize the subjectivies of students has been addressed in the work of a variety of critical educational theorists. (Apple, 1979; Bourdieu and Passeron, 1977; Freire, 1971; 1985; Giroux, 1981; 1983; Willis, 1977) Perhaps the most influential of these theorists has been Freire. His insistence on the necessity of dialogue between teacher and students as subjects has influenced the works of a number of educators who have attempted to create liberating ways of teaching. (Shor, 1980; Frankenstein, 1983) In Freire's pedagogy, students must embark upon the process of investigating those historical processes that have led to their class, gender, and race interests and power. They explore both their oppression and their power in the light of moral and political questions of justice and equality. But teachers are also subjects, with historically situated interests. Teachers also draw upon power according to their race and gender in their interaction in the classroom. (Walkerdine, 1981) If they are feminist teachers, their goals of addressing sexist oppression may conflict with their students on a variety of levels. The feminist woman teacher faces the resistance and use of male privilege in boys, who of course have a vested interest in maintaining their own gender privilege, particularly if they face race or class oppression. But she may also meet students, both boys and girls, whose class cultures present gender differences in ways that are deeply opposed to what may be the middle-class culture of the feminist teacher. And if the teacher is white, she must be conscious that she may symbolize racist oppression to her black students. Thus the feminist teacher who seeks to demystify and combat sexism finds herself in a social site in which conflicting demands of class and race also are part of her own and her students' subjectivities. The feminist teacher who seeks to oppose sexism in her teaching must become clear about her own class and race subjectivity in her relationships in the classroom.

As we have seen in the life histories and work experiences of these women teachers, gender is highly significant for them precisely *because* they have experienced sexist oppression in a variety of ways and at different points in their lives. Men have no need to define themselves by their gender; a man, for example, does not identify himself as a male administrator, because that is the norm. But since all women are in some way oppressed by sexism, they are conscious of their identity as women in a way that men rarely are as men. Thus one major focus of their teaching in the feminist classroom is to address issues of sexism, to challenge sexist assumptions, and to reveal gender discrimination and oppression. As one of these teachers commented:

> You look back on your own socialization and your own kind of intellectual training and you realize that so much of it was missing because no one ever thought of teaching it then. And [you want] to be sort of sure that's not going to happen again.

While these women teachers are particularly conscious of sexism because of their own subjectivity as women, they are also conscious of the class and race identities of their students. As we have seen, in interviews they spoke of the need to recognize their students' own cultural worlds and to respect the validity of that culture. As one of the women administrators put it, otherwise teachers can be "an affront" to students and their families. Throughout these discussions, the teachers talked of raising questions and making the students more self-conscious about racism and sexism while respecting their own cultural worlds. They defined their work as providing a place where students could interrogate their own accepted beliefs and identities; they defined teaching not as the transmission of a static "knowledge," what Freire refers to as banking education, but as an expansion of accepted discourse both about society as a whole and about the subjective experiences of students.

It is one thing to have goals and a vision of what education should be like; it is another thing to be able to accomplish that vision in the realities of the classroom in which the gender, race, and class sub-jectivities of teachers and students come directly into conflict. The feminist views of teachers create tensions and conflicts in the class-room as meaning is negotiated, imposed, and resisted by teachers and students of different subjectivities. In this chapter, the complexity of conflicting gender, race, and class subjectivities is examined by looking at the classroom practice of feminist teachers and the re-sponses to their teaching by students of a variety of different subjectivities.

## GENDER, RACE, AND CLASS IN CLASSROOM DISCOURSE

Feminist teaching in a public high school takes place within the culture of the wider school, and the institutional structure itself limits and shapes classroom discourse. The rigid structure of the school day, with 45-minute classes, the physical structure of the classroom itself, with its blackboard at the front of the room and the teacher's large desk, the bureaucratic paper work of grades given four times a year, profoundly shape relationships between students and teachers. Students come to a class as only one of seven classes they take throughout the day and they have certain expectations of teacher authority and classroom behavior that cannot be simply erased when they walk into a particular teacher's class. And the teacher herself knows the need to retain authority and to achieve goals, both her own and the goals of the institution, which she must meet if she is to retain her job.

Within these structural limits, feminist teachers attempt to challenge their students' accepted beliefs and lived relationships. In their prac-tice, they attempt to realize what they see as their goals as feminist teachers. In this chapter, the difficulty of achieving these goals in multicultural and mixed-class public school settings is illuminated through an examination of classroom discourse. By examining the classrooms of feminist teachers, the complexity of this interaction between students and teachers is highlighted. In these classrooms, the feminist goals of the teachers are made clear to students through subject matter and direct statements on the part of the teachers. But the responses to this feminist content and practice varies widely ac-cording to the gender, class, and race of the students in the classroom. The teacher's meaning is both affirmed and contested by different students. Thus both the possibilities of and obstacles to counter-hegemonic teaching are revealed in these classrooms.

Classroom discourse reveals meaning mutually created by teachers and students. It is never neutral, but is always situated in the context of a socially and historically defined present. Teachers and students use language to assert their own power and to try to create sense for themselves out of a complex social setting. As Bakhtin reminds us:

> Language is not a neutral medium that passes freely and easily into the private property of the speaker's intentions; it is populated—overpopulated—with the intentions of others. Expropriating it, forcing it to submit to one's own intentions and accents, is a difficult and complicated process. (Bakhtin, 1981, p. 294)

Official classroom discourse is dominated by the intentions of teachers; they set subjects, assign texts, ask questions about texts, and assert their ultimate authority through testing. But the discourse of the classroom is not completely controlled by them. There is a "sub rosa" discourse in classrooms, made up of both verbal and nonverbal communication among students. (Gilmore, 1983) As Bennett and Sola point out, this sub rosa discourse may well be "created out of different needs than those defined by the school—and the groups that govern schooling in this country—as legitimate." (Bennett and Sola, 1985, p. 93) Teachers need to recognize the intentions of students and seek to legitimate those intentions through the expansion of official classroom discourse. But that legitimation on the part of teachers will depend greatly on whether or not there is a "fit" between the intentions of the teacher and those of the students. (Bennett and Sola, 1985) The possibilities of that fit, a basis of shared values and assumptions, depends upon the subjectivities of teachers as well as students. Moreover, students in any classroom may themselves come into conflict with one another because of their own different ethnic, class, and gender subjectivities. And as Bakhtin emphasizes, each individual's subjectivity itself is constantly being redefined as meaning is asserted, contested, affirmed, or denied.

In the following discussion I have drawn upon incidents from the classrooms of a number of white, middle-class teachers who were articulate and positive about their feminist beliefs. While in many respects it might be preferable to analyze in depth the work of specific teachers in classrooms, the question of confidentiality, preventing the possibilty that discussions of a teacher's practice could in some way be used to their disadvantage, seems to me the researcher's first responsibility. (See Connell, 1985) Thus I have not presented case studies of individual teachers. Instead, I have used examples of discourse from a number of classrooms with varying student populations. I have included examples from classrooms of the school-within-a-school in the more middle-class high school and examples from the more working-class and ethnically mixed high school. Students gained admission to the school-within-a-school through a lottery and competition was strong among middle-class parents to get their children into the school, which was perceived by them to be the most desirable program at the high school. Thus the students in school-within-a-school courses were already to some extent self-selected. The curriculum was organized around a series of electives and included courses on "women's studies" in both social studies and literature. The classes I observed at the other site were part of the curriculum of the regular high school and were not part of a special program. This second school was in general more mixed in terms of class and ethnicity. The classes I observed in this high school were not labeled "women's studies"; some were required courses and some were electives, but all of them were more mixed than the school-within-a-school classes in terms of class background and ethnicity of students. While these settings do not represent rigid class and race divisions, the classrooms described here do represent examples of a variety of class- and ethnically- (as well as gender) based values and attitudes on the part of students.

While all the teachers here were clear about their feminist beliefs and antisexist (and antiracist) goals of their teaching, the subjects they taught were not usually defined as women's subjects. As public school teachers, they had to teach literature, composition, U.S. history, humanities, etc. The students in these courses were not self-selected in terms of their interest or concern with feminist issues and represented a wide variety of class, ethnic, and gender interests. Courses labeled "women's studies" were electives at the school-within-a-school which attracted a certain kind of student—primarily white, middle-class girls with feminist mothers. The interaction in these classrooms, as we will see, could be quite different from the interaction in mixed-gender, mixed-class classrooms taught by feminist teachers.

Classroom observation presented certain unavoidable problems of observer and observed. At the beginning of my observations, I felt that my presence in the classroom affected both teacher and students. And while students seemed to become used to me sitting in the back of the room with my notebook, I felt the teachers *always* were aware of me. One teacher confirmed this later in an interview, in which she said that any observer made her nervous. It seems to me that this must be true of any observer in a classroom, but unfortunely, except for hidden observation posts or hidden cameras (which raise certain ethical and political issues I should hope would prevent their use) there is no way to observe classroom discourse without being an observer, and thus influencing what occurs. This influence must be acknowledged, and we have to assume that the interaction and issues that emerge in observed classroom discourse are representative and can be interrogated and analyzed and that they do reveal the dynamics of the classroom.

Feminist teachers attempt to achieve their goals through both texts and classroom practices. Through these means, they redefine what Johnson has called "useful knowledge." (Johnson, 1980) They take two interrelated approaches that I think are essential to the kind of critical feminist teaching they hope to achieve. First, they expand the limits of discourse, by directly addressing the forces that shape their students' lives. As teachers, within the scope of the curriculum and the structure of the school, they select topics for discussion and study, but they also attempt to legitimize their students' voices by acknowledging their students' own experiences and by calling for their students' own narratives. They frequently comment directly on classroom interaction and attempt to create relationships within the class that challenge accepted behavior and attitudes of men and women. Second, and related to the expansion of discourse, is their own presentation of themselves as gendered subjects with a personal perspective on issues of gender and race. They are overtly political in their presentation and both will use personal anecdotes and will challenge and engage students on these topics. Thus they reveal their own subjectivity and interests, while at the same time within certain limits legitimating the subjectivity of their students. The overt statement of feminist interests, however, can either affirm students (most frequently white middle-class girls from feminist homes) or it can conflict with students along gender, class, or race lines. The contradictory ways these texts and practices are read by students can be seen in the discourse in these classrooms.

Courses in women's studies are constructed to address issues of sexism directly. These classrooms were dominated by white middle-class girls. In these courses, both the subject matter of the course and the teachers' presentation were overtly directed as an attack on sexist oppression. An example of this can be seen from a women's studies course at the school-within-a-school in two classes I observed on women in advertising. Students read two magazine articles dealing with commercial images of women and ideals of beauty. In the first class, the teacher had students list men and women they admired as beautiful. From these lists, she then pointed out that for women, the ideal was to be white, blonde, tall, young, and thin, and that the women mentioned were admired primarily for the way they looked. The men mentioned, on the other hand, were actors or sports figures, and included a much wider range of ages, races, and physical types. For the next class, she had students bring in three advertisements offensive to women or stereotyping women. In this class, the students passed around their own ads and the teacher also shared some she had collected, which included a large number of sadomasochistic ads. As she passed these around, the teacher said, "you need to start to be conscious about what they're doing." She held up two Levis ads, one for boys' and one for girls' jeans, and asked the students to note "the bum shots" in the ads for girls' jeans. Throughout her discussion, she was direct in her condemnation of advertising for its exploitation of women's bodies and its "cooptation of the women's movement." In this class, the teacher talked most of the time; the students, largely white middle-class girls, responded by occasional words or groans of agreement. This teacher, who teaches courses in both the school-within-a-school and in the "regular" streams in this high school, recognizes the relative ease of teaching the material in this setting:

> It's easy to teach a course dealing with issues of sexism to these kids because they're middle-class kids, because it's an issue at home. You know, their mothers are usually feminists and you can hear that, I'm sure you've heard that in the class this week, this is what my mother does, that kind of thing. Whereas with working-class kids you have to be much more sensitive that the kids can take it as a criticism of their culture.

In a "social problems" class in the second high school, which is much more mixed in terms of race and gender, the teacher deals directly with social relationships and identity. She is also conscious of the nature of her classroom and the subjectivities of her students around gender and race:

> I think that high school boys are as chauvinistic as it's possible to be. They can't get any worse than they are right now. I think the interesting thing to me in terms of the racial thing is that black female students seem most of the time to be very aware of these things, maybe because they're already aware of discrimination.

This teacher's own strong consciousness of sexism and her anger at oppression and inequality is clearly expressed in her teaching. In teaching about social class and status, she addresses the issue of men's and women's jobs:

> Teacher: Is there a difference between waiter and waitress?
> Various voices: Yes!
> Teacher: The higher class the restaurant, the more likely they are to have ...
> Various voices: Men!
> Teacher: Right!

This class was not defined as a women's studies course, but this teacher consistently raised issues of sexist oppression, both in her handling of the subject matter and in her questioning of classroom social relationships. She made her own position clear and would challenge students when she disagreed with them. She also supported girls in classroom discussion. Here is part of the discussion of the status of various jobs:

> Teacher: What conclusions?
> White girl: The highest paying jobs are at the top.
> White boy: Not really. Policeman is there.
> White girl: Yeah, you're right.
> Teacher: Don't back down just because he disagrees with you!

In this example the teacher intervened on the part of the girl and in so doing makes classroom discourse a part of her text. By calling attention to the way in which the girl backs down and accepts the boy's suggestion of policemen, she raises to consciousness the gendered quality of these attitudes and interactions. Because of the presence of a sizable number of boys in this social studies class, the teacher's critique of sexist social relationships and practices raised conflicts that did not occur in the women's studies classes, which tended to be made up largely of middle-class girls with a positive view of feminism.

The teacher of this high school social problems class also addresses accepted gender roles in the organization of her classroom. She frequently breaks her class into groups to discuss texts or films they have seen. This is one recognized way to try to break down a teacher-centered classroom. But this particular teacher also addresses the common situation in which boys either dominate discussion or "opt out" of the assignment while girls dutifully fulfill what is asked. She requires boys to be secretaries and girls to be spokespersons for each group. She will divide the class into groups that will be balanced according to gender for this purpose. This teacher feels girls appreciate this redefinition of roles, although the boys are not so enthusiastic. As this teacher comments:

> The male secretary, that really drives them up the wall, and they forget about it until the next time. It's like, she's going to do that again, I know she is! But it's been interesting ... it's amazing how good the females feel about that, for once in their lives not to be expected to be the secretary. I've had several students over the years come up to me and say, very explicitly, Hey, that made me feel good. To have somebody finally realize that I am always stuck with taking notes.

This teacher sees this practice as one way she forces students out of accepted relationships and thus calls into question the dominant/subordinate gender relationships to which they are accustomed.

The boys in her classes accepted this practice grudgingly. In one class, when this teacher split the class into groups and then reminded them that a boy must be secretary, one boy replied, "You make me feel like a piece of meat, Ms.————." The teacher smiled and did not reply. When the groups came back together to report on their discussion, there was this interchange between the teacher and this boy:

> Teacher: Remember that the female must be the spokesperson.
> Boy: You know, you really *like* to say that.
> Teacher: I think it's a nice set up.

This interchange continued as the teacher asked the groups to combine items together into categories:

> Boy: She wants women!
> Teacher: No, no, no. Stop picking on me.

This teacher mentioned later that she always tries to split groups up so there will be at least two boys in each group, "so they will have to fight about who has to be secretary."

The boys in this social problems class mentioned this practice of having boys be secretaries later in a class discussion I held with this class about their teacher's teaching methods. For them, it was a case of "reverse discrimination." I asked the class what they felt their teacher's attitude toward women and women's issues was:

> White boy #1: She favors 'em.
> White boy #2: Greatly.
> Black girl: I don't think she favors them. I think she goes about it fairly but you can see a little bit of favoritism toward women. I'm not saying . . . because she *is* a woman, she favors them more.
> White boy #1: She retaliates by discriminating against us males.
> (Girls laugh)
> White boy #2: She's not that bad.
> White boy #1: When we split into groups, a male has to be secretary of the group.
> White boy #2: Yes, and a female *has* to be the spokes*person.* She's an extremist in some sense.
> White boy #2: That's reverse discrimination.
> Black girl: I don't think it's discrimination.
> White girl: That's because you're males.
> Black girl: I think if she graded them tougher . . .
> White boy #2: Well, she doesn't.
> Black girl: I think when she does that, well, me as a woman, I feel that she gives us a chance to have a chance to talk. Usually when you're with a group of men you don't have a chance. And then with a boy, you don't usually see a male secretary, you don't see a male nurse, and it's just a

way of showing us that there can be a male secretary and there can be a female spokesperson.

White boy: She told us, usually the girls do all the writing and the males take all the credit.

Other feminist teachers also come into conflict with the boys in their classes. One teacher describes her relationship with a ninth grade class in social studies at the high school:

> I'm just having a big brawl with my freshmen, sort of an ongoing brawl, I should say, because the class is pretty much polarized sex-wise as 14-year-olds can be. The boys, a lot of kids, are from [the vocational program] so they're sort of into the macho falseness that they're trying to cultivate. And they just get on me all the time, accusing me of favoring the girls, to which my response is, I think they *should* be favored. And kind of raising the issue of, well, why do you think they're favored? Is this a new experience? To the girls, Do you like being favored?

In this class, a group of working-class boys challenges the teacher for what they perceive as her feminist bias. She responds by affirming her support of the girls and her identification with the girls' interests. Once again, the teacher has made accepted gender roles problematic and has made the social relationships of the classroom itself part of her text for teaching.

All of these feminist teachers incorporate struggles over gender and attacks on sexism in the content of their teaching and the social relationships of the classroom. They also use their own experiences and identities as feminists by relating personal experiences and by making their own moral judgments and political positions overt. Thus in a women's studies class at the school-within-a-school, one teacher used her own childhood experience of her brother having been given an Erector set which she always played with. This teacher claims she was good at math as a result, unlike most young girls who are not encouraged to work with construction kinds of toys. The students in the class responded to her story:

> Girl: Does a boy get limited too if he just gets masculine toys?
> Teacher: You answer that.
> Girl: I guess they don't learn verbal things. It's a bad deal for boys, they have all these pent up feelings.
> Girl #2: When I have kids, I'm going to give them Slinkies.

One of the striking aspects of this use of personal anecdote and political statement is the alliance that is set up between the feminist teacher and middle-class girls.

Here is an interchange in a U.S. history elective taught by a feminist teacher at the school-within-a-school, a class made up largely of white,

middle-class students. The students have been reading Philip Caputo's
*Rumors of War* and are discussing whether atrocities could be
justified:

> Boy: Yes [atrocities are justified] if it will help you through the war.
> Boy #2: If they kill your friend, it's okay.
> Girl: No. They think it's like a football game.
> Teacher: Is that the American mind set? Is it moral?
> Boy #1: No, but it's gone on so long.
> Girl: Those Marines seemed to forget what's right and what's wrong.
> Boy #2: Look at My Lai. An officer shot himself in the foot. One officer, one
> enlisted man refused.
> Girl: It's the male ego.
> Teacher: I'm hearing different things from boys and girls.
>
> *****
>
> Boy # 1: Girls can't serve in the army because they will always be brushing
> their hair.
> Teacher: Oh, I won't let you get away with that, that's a sexual stereotype.
> Boy #1: Well, if you accuse me of machoism . . .
> Teacher: Oh, we outnumber you guys.

This teacher then goes on to analyze the connection between war and
male values. When she finishes, she says, "Case finished," and the
girls in the class break into applause. In this exchange, the teacher
guides the conversation to a consideration of male and female values
by saying early on, "I seem to be hearing different things from girls
and boys." In this way she makes conscious the gendered discourse
of the classroom. Later, when the boy makes the remark about girls
not being in the army because they would be brushing their hair, she
names his statement a "sexual stereotype." And then in the exchange,
she overtly identifies her own gender with the girls in the class through
using "we" ("Oh, we outnumber you guys"). In this way, she is not a
neutral facilitator in the classroom, but has identified her own interests
and thus intervenes in a gender conflict on the side of the girls and
in opposition to the boys. This is precisely what the other teacher is
doing in her exchanges with boys over the male secretary. This kind
of interchange occurred over and over again in all of these feminist
teachers' classrooms. For students who shared their criticisms of sexism, this kind of teaching was an affirmation of their own views and
their own identities. As white middle-class feminists, teachers were
clear about their own interests, interests which reflected their own
subjectivities. But of course, by no means all of the students in these
high schools were white, middle-class women.

   The feminist teacher who is calling into question accepted beliefs
and attitudes about gender no more imposes her own meaning and

culture upon the classroom than does the traditional teacher who wants students to accept authority and the status quo. In all these classrooms, meaning is negotiated and contested by teachers and students with very different class, gender, and race histories and relationships. As Giroux comments, we need to

> account theoretically for the ways in which language, ideology, history, and experience come together to produce, define, and constrain particular forms of teacher-student practice ... power and discourse are now investigated not merely as the homogeneous echo of the logic of capital, but as a polyphony of voices mediated within different layers of reality shaped through an interaction of dominant and subordinate forms of power. (Giroux, 1985, p. 6)

Thus the classroom is always a site of conflict, and will be a site of conflict for the feminist or critical teacher trying to create a counter-hegemonic vision just as much as it will be for a traditional or authoritarian teacher. This is precisely because students are agents and creators of meaning in both settings. The dominant and subordinate forms of power that Giroux mentions are not simply the dominance of the teacher and the subordination of the student. Students also are gendered, raced, and classed; they therefore "read" texts and classroom social relationships according to those subjectivities.

As we have seen, one clear source of conflict in the feminist classroom is that based on gender. The teacher is a woman, and thus must struggle against a subordinate subjectivity in a patriarchal society; the male student as a male has experienced a dominant subjectivity in his family, in the images of the media, and in the ways he has experienced authority in the wider society. But in the classroom, the teacher has the power of authority and the male student is subordinate as student. These parameters of power lead to the tensions we noted above. But these conflicts are not simply based on gender conflicts between women teachers and boys, but also emerge from the conflict of gender expectations in class and ethnic cultures.

The patriarchal nature of the ethnic cultures of many students at both schools was mentioned in interviews by both teachers and administrators. This conflict between class cultures and feminism is illustrated in a school-within-a-school women's studies class. This class was dominated by white middle-class girls. There were also two working-class white girls in the class. On this day, the class was discussing a notorious rape trial that had just ended. In this case, a young Portuguese woman was gang raped in a bar by a group of Portuguese immigrant men. In the trial, she was accused of acting in a provocative way because she had come into a bar where there were no other women, she had quite a few drinks, and had left her children at home alone. The men were convicted of raping her and were sentenced to long prison terms. This discussion took place at the beginning of a class period later in the term. The students were discussing the woman's action in going into the bar. Marie, although not Portuguese, was a white working-class girl; Jessica's parents were professionals and her mother was a feminist:

> Marie: That woman tells so many stories . . .
> Janet: In the beginning, the one that was crying, he confessed.
> Teacher: Then he retracted that.
> Marie: Then you figure, she left her kids at home, went to get cigarets . . .
> Jessica: So what if she flirted, got drinks, whatever, it's totally irrelevant. If they forced themselves on her, it's rape.
> Marie: Well, she could have forced herself on them.
> Other girls: Oh come on . . . (groans)
> Teacher: It doesn't matter what kind of person she was, she has the right to keep her humanity. This happens over and over again, that the woman has to defend her character.
> Jessica: Isn't this a case where there was a protest that they convicted them just because they were Portuguese?
> Janet: Yeah but the woman, the cops were also Portuguese.
>
> *****
>
> Teacher: This is an interesting question. Whether immigrants are treated differently. But also that working-class girls deserve this if they don't act right. The connotation is, since she's not a nice girl, she deserves it. To me, that's disturbing.
> Jessica: So they think it's okay that she was raped, because she's not a nice person.

The teacher's involvement in this discussion was to support and elaborate on the view of Jessica, who throughout the course presented a strong feminist point of view. Thus Jessica's discourse was legitimated and supported. However, Marie, who was one of the few working-class students in the class, was dismissed and in a sense delegitimated. Eventually in this discussion Jessica and the teacher confirmed their similar view of the rape trial, while Marie sank into silence with a frown.

In this interchange, a feminist viewpoint was affirmed and classroom discourse expanded to include contemporary examples of sexism as a legitimate topic of discussion. For students who agree with this view, the classroom becomes a place where their own views are confirmed and their subjectivities are recognized. But for the working-class girl, classroom discourse once again imposes a set of values and attitudes that are foreign to her. This teacher feels strongly that women should not be blamed for being raped and she used her superior knowledge and ability to argue to defend Jessica and elaborate on her argument. In so doing, she challenged sexist views that women deserve rape because of their "provocative" behavior. But for Marie, the working-class girl, once again middle-class discourse has controlled the classroom. For her, the issue was not only sexism, it was also classism. This is a good example of what Bakhtin means by the "intentions" of discourse. In condemning the sexism of these views on rape, the teacher called upon her authority as the teacher to legitimate and express a particular view, one, I am sure, she would defend, and one with which I would certainly agree. But in the context of classroom discourse, Marie's intentions and the cultural context from which she spoke were not addressed. Thus in this instance, the power of class is used to attack the oppression of sexism, but the working-class girl is caught in between.

Another source of conflict for the white feminist is that based on race. As a white person in a racist society, she is privileged and has experienced herself as dominant. She may oppose racism in her personal life and in her teaching, but to the black student, she can represent white domination and thus may be resisted and struggled against. The black boy then can call upon his dominant position as a male in a sexist society to oppose her power as white in a racist society. Thus these two forms of oppression come into conflict. When that conflict occurs, the white woman teacher may fall back on her dominance in the teacher/student relationship. This kind of conflict is apparent in this exchange in a social studies class in the second high school. This class was almost exactly split between black and white students, and the majority of the students were from working-class families.

In this class, the teacher was using the passage from Malcolm X's autobiography in which his teacher, Mr. Ostrowski, talks to him about his future. Here is a selection from that text:

He told me, "Malcolm, you ought to be thinking about a career. Have you been giving it thought?"

The truth is, I hadn't. I never have figured out why I told him, "Well, yes, sir, I've been thinking I'd like to be a lawyer." Lansing certainly had no Negro lawyers—or doctors either—in those days, to hold up an image I might have aspired to. All I really knew for certain was that a lawyer didn't wash dishes, as I was doing.

Mr. Ostrowski looked surprised, I remember, and leaned back in his chair and clasped his hands behind his back. He kind of half smiled and said: "Malcolm, one of life's first needs is for us to be realistic. Don't misunderstand me, now. We all here like you, you know that. But you've got to be realistic about being a nigger. A lawyer—that's no realistic goal for a nigger. You need to think about something you can be. You're good with your hands—making things. Everybody admires your carpentry shop work. Why don't you plan on carpentry. People like you as a person—you'd get all kinds of work."

The more I thought afterward about what he said, the more uneasy it made me . . . I was smarter than nearly all those white kids. But apparently I was still not intelligent enough in his eyes, to become whatever I wanted to be. It was then that I began to change— inside.

I drew away from white people.

The teacher used this passage to discuss the way that people build a self-image from the way their identity is reflected in the opinions and attitudes of others. In the class this day (about two weeks into the semester) was a new black boy, John. He had joined this already-established class at the beginning of the semester. The teacher passed out the passage and had the students read it silently. After reading it, John sat back, sighed, began tapping his fingers loudly on the desk.

Teacher: What was Mr. Ostrowski telling him?
Black girl: He knew you couldn't have black lawyers back then.
John: (interrupts) He's indirectly telling him to change his goals. Because he's a *nigger*.
Teacher: He's being told to be realistic . . .
John: Hold on. This is prejudice. At that particular time, prejudice was rife then.
Teacher: What image is he picking up here?
John: Negative.
White boy: His character was such that he saw it as a challenge.

*****

[The teacher then goes on to say that Malcolm became a black nationalist and a separatist]
Teacher: We do not have to accept the image other people give of us.
John: Mr. Ostrowski was threatened by the black guy's motivation, that the black guy's aiming high.
Teacher: Okay, we're not talking about Mr. Ostrowski right now . . .

The teacher then began guiding the class to consider the concept of "significant others," the sources of people's self-concept, motivation, internalized sense of themselves. Throughout, John tapped his fingers on the desk, sighed, moved his chair. The teacher guided the discussion away from racism and toward various theories of socialization.

When I talked to the teacher the next day I discovered that John had dropped the class, much to her relief. She found this particular class a "very positive" group, and saw John's behavior and comments as disruptive, aggressive, and seemingly directed at her personally. In the way he restlessly moved his chair, sighed, and tapped his fingers in the classroom, he clearly communicated his boredom or anger at what was going on in the class, and he thus became defined for the teacher as a "discipline problem." But of course it is also possible to look at his comments as his own appropriation of meaning as he read the passage by Malcolm X. For him, the significant category was racism, not socialization; for him the teacher was a white authority who *should* be challenged ("Hold on. This is prejudice . . .").

The conflict in this case is based on race, and the conflict is between the authority of the white woman teacher and the resistance of the black male student. The text from Malcolm X's autobiography was being read in two different ways by teacher and student. For the teacher, the text was part of a discourse she had clearly established in her own mind. This particular class was part of a larger structure of knowledge and meaning; she wanted to develop a theory of socialization in order to build theoretical knowledge she would then use in the rest of the course. But for John, the passage had meaning out of his own experience of racism as a black boy in a racist society. His discourse was one of lived racism, not an academic discourse. Within the context of the classroom, his statements (both verbal and nonverbal) were read by the teacher as a disruption of the academic discourse and structure of knowledge she was trying to introduce to the class as a whole. For her, John was disrupting what she experienced as a very positive and successful classroom relationship. And this teacher was respected and well liked by both black and white students in the class, judging from my observation and from comments on questionnaires I passed out at the end of this course. There were several other instances in my observation of this class that showed her strong support for black students and her own awareness of and condemnation of racism. It is easy to criticize the teacher in this case for not recognizing John's subjectivity, but it is important not to read this example as one of "individual failure" on the part of the teacher. Instead, this incident illuminates the ways in which texts and classroom discourse are read from the perspectives of different socially defined subjectivities. For the teacher, this incident illustrates the complexities and difficulties of mediating and recognizing conflicting meanings in the midst of classroom discourse. This incident could be and *was* read differently and had different meaning depending on the subjectivity and interests of those involved.

Conflicts based on race also occur between students as well. Black students, for example, may expand the range of discourse in ways that white students and white teachers may not be conscious of because of their own white subjectivity. Here is an example in a feminist teacher's class in which the teacher accepts and incorporates the black student's voice. This women's studies class at the school-within-a-school has been discussing the nature of women's history. The teacher passes out a poem, "A story simple and complicated," which ends:

> We cry at the knowledge that many of our mothers are lost to us forever
> ... unwritten unspoken unheard unsung, though unimportant ...
> We ask you to unite with us in thoughts of restoration
> of a Herstory for all women to be part of
> in the now
>   in the yesterday
>     in the times to be.

> White boy: What is Herstory?
> White girl: His story
> Teacher: Who writes the history?
> White girl: Men.
> Black girl: White men.

The teacher responds to this remark by telling a story of a friend of hers who refused to use a book because it failed to discuss Africa. She then asks the students what they study when they study U.S. history. They cite "Columbus, the Mayflower, the Indians, Pocahontas, Priscilla and John, the Revolution, the slave trade (White girl: "A triangle, we had to draw a triangle"), the Civil War." In the subsequent discussion, the teacher points out that not only are women unrepresented in this history, but so largely are "blacks, Indians and others who don't have a voice." In her discussion, then, the teacher legitimates and acknowledges the comment of the black girl that it's not just that men write history, but that it's white men who do so. In this way the discourse of race as well as gender (which was the teacher's intention) is incorporated into what is legitimate to say and think in the classroom.

The incorporation of race and racism into classroom discourse is not always as smooth as this example. In the case above, the students were largely middle class and there was only one black student, a girl whose mother was a feminist and ran a shelter for battered women. Alone, she did not threaten to dominate classroom discourse. The situation was different in classes which were split much more evenly according to race. Here is a description of a social studies class at the second high school. This class included eight black girls, four white girls, two black boys and six white boys. In this class, the black girls were articulate and often contributed to class discussion. At the beginning of one class, the teacher began by mentioning that students from two nearby high schools were coming to visit the high school and this social studies class on Friday:

Black girl #1: I went to [Madison] High last year. There were about six minorities and the [Madison] kids acted real stupid, there were fights and stuff. [Jackson] doesn't like minorities at all. I have a cousin that goes and gets hassled all the time.

Black girl #2: But it's not as bad as [Jefferson].

Teacher: I had a student who had to take the bus to work near [Jefferson]. But I thought [Jackson] was lessened somewhat.

Black girl #1: When I went to [Madison] High I thought it wouldn't be that bad. But I went to a chemistry class and all they did was throw airplanes ...

Teacher: [Jackson] is a very poor, tight, ethnic community.

Black girl #2: What are they? Irish, Polish? They always stick together.

Throughout this exchange between the two black girls and the teacher, four white boys across the room talk together in moderately loud voices about other topics. Finally the teacher turns to them and calls their names.

White boy: (with exaggerated politeness): Excuse me?

The teacher and the black girls continue to talk about racism in the city and in various schools, but the white boys do not enter into the conversation.

In this exchange, the teacher legitimates the voices of the black girls by entering into a discussion that they largely initiate and by acknowledging the existence of racism. The resistance to this discourse then comes from the white boys, possibly on grounds of race, possibly on grounds of gender. For the teacher, legitimating the voices of the black girls then leads to conflicts with the white boys. In later classes, these same boys never refer to the black girls by name, but will only say "like *she* said" if they want to respond to a black girl.

## CONCLUSION

The classroom entered by the feminist, antiracist woman teacher is not a neutral environment in which knowledge can be controlled and communicated to a blank audience. She meets and speaks with students who carry with them kinds of knowledge, ways of relating to one another, values, experiences of oppression or privilege that have deeply affected and defined them. While the teacher has access to the power of judgment (marking) and the weight of the institution, she is at the same time fixed according to race and gender and thus participates in dominant/subordinate relationships with students in these terms. What we see in the classroom are complex redefinitions and constructions of meaning, conflicts between different loci of power that have their root in the class, race, and gender divisions of U.S. society as a whole.

In these feminist-taught classrooms, we can see the ways that gender, class, and race subjectivities lead to different readings of classroom discourse and different forms of resistance on the part of students. The feminist teacher cannot escape her own gender, class, and race identity as she interacts with students in the classroom. Both her political and personal beliefs and her own subjectivity will be read and responded to differently by different students. Thus a white feminist teacher may affirm the subjectivities of her white, middle-class girl students. The nature of the discourse between them is often one of mutual affirmation. As in the discussion between the teacher and Jessica about the rape trial, the dialogue is a give and take of shared assumptions and social vision. But as we saw in the case of Marie, the working-class girl in that discussion, not all girl students will find feminism an affirmation. It may be a threat to their class or ethnic identity. The conflict between feminist women teachers and boy students is more predictable and most obvious. In this case, feminist teachers make that conflict a part of their conscious teaching; it becomes a kind of text. They challenge boys about their gender privilege and intervene on the part of the girls. Perhaps most complex is the relationship of race. As we saw, in one case a teacher legitimated and supported the black girls in their discussion of racism and schools. But in the case of John and his reading of Malcolm X, the teacher's authority was called upon to delegitimate his reading, which was based precisely on his subjectivity as a black boy.

In these feminist teachers' classrooms, we can see the "multi-layered" quality of both students and teachers as subjects. In examining these classrooms, it is important to recognize the ways in which feminist teachers make existing social relationships problematic and make conscious sexist ideology and practices. In their teaching practice, feminist teachers challenge male hegemony and expand the limits of classroom discourse to include a discussion of the power and oppression experienced by both boys and girls in their everyday lives as gendered subjects. But their teaching also leads to conflicts between the essentially middle-class subjectivity of the teacher and the working-class and ethnic cultures of her students. The feminist teacher affirms the experiences of her girl students, but challenges the privilege of the boys. And white teachers have to recognize the implicit power of their whiteness.

In cases where the gender, race, or class of teacher and student are different, feminist teaching creates conflicts on various levels. But that conflict can become the text for counter-hegemonic teaching. What is important is not to deny conflict, but to recognize that in a society like the U.S., which is so deeply split by gender, race, and class, conflict is inevitable and only reflects social and political realities. But recognition of conflict, oppression, and power does not mean their acceptance. It means making them conscious so they can be addressed and transformed. Feminist teachers, if they are to work to create a counter-hegemonic teaching, must be conscious of their own gendered, classed, and raced subjectivities as they confirm or challenge the lived experiences of their students. This does not mean avoiding or denying conflict, but legitimating this polyphony of voices and making both our oppression and our power conscious in the discourse of the classroom.

# 7

# Conclusion

*Only beings who can reflect upon the fact that they are determined are capable of freeing themselves.*

—*Paulo Freire*

THROUGHOUT THIS STUDY I have tried to explore the dynamics between the power of structural determinants and the consciousness of individuals who can become aware of those determinants, and thus attempt to change them. The focus of this study was on feminist teachers and administrators who work in the public schools. In examining their lives and work, I think we can see the tension between the power of institutions, which have been created under particular historical, economic, and social conditions, and the will of individuals, who may be in opposition to those forces, and who themselves can influence the present structure of the institutions. There is, as we have seen, a constant interplay or dialectic between the two: the historically formed and institutionally limited individuals, and the humanly created and defined institutions.

In the early theoretical chapters, I discussed this dialectic as one of the major concerns of contemporary philosophy and social theory. In philosophy, this tension is expressed as that between structure and agency; in critical educational theory, it has been approached through the opposing paradigms of reproduction and resistance. As we have seen in the lives and work of these feminist teachers and administrators, both ways of viewing social reality are necessary. As Freire comments, individuals *are* determined, but they are also able to reflect on that determination and thus begin to "free themselves." I have argued throughout that while it is important not to ignore the power of political and economic forces and history as determinants, it is at least as important for thinking about political work in schools to see and consider the agency and will of both teachers and students. Only in this way can we see the possibilities of the classroom.

Teachers are not simply parts of some mechanism of social reproduction; nor are their lives dictated by the demands of capital, racism, or patriarchy in such a way that they are mere automatons. Teachers are actors and agents in complex social sites where social forces powerfully shape the limits of what is possible. But these teachers retain the ability to be conscious and to analyze and act within this socially defined site. In this way, they are intellectuals and act as intellectuals to critique and attempt to transform the social world they inhabit. Because of my own interest in these teachers and administrators as women, I focused on their practice as women who struggle against patriarchal hegemony and who seek to encourage among students a critical consciousness of sexism and the roles of men and women. But as became clear to me and as I think is evident in these accounts, their practice moves beyond a concentration on feminist issues alone. Instead, we see, in classroom interactions and in their own accounts of their goals, a recognition of the overlapping oppressions of race, ethnicity, and class. In their work, they seek to create classrooms that encourage critique on the part of students in relation to a number of different forms of oppression.

In these schools and the classrooms of these feminist teachers, the complexity of social sites in which individuals of different class, race, and gender subjectivites come together is illuminated. These schools are not isolated from the dynamics of the wider society; quite the contrary, they magnify the contradictions and tensions of a society so marked by inequality and oppression. In these classrooms, individual students and teachers make "sense" of classroom discourse according to their own histories and social location. In many respects, what happens in these classrooms is a kind of negotiation of competing oppressions and power, as individuals use—often unconsciously—their own power to make sense of, appropriate, or reject the situation. Because of the conflicts among them in terms of gender, race, and class, it is inevitable that these classrooms are marked by tension and conflicts, as the competing subjectivities of teacher and students come into play. In fact, it is precisely because the goal of feminist teachers is to raise questions and to make their classrooms places where accepted social reality can be questioned that allows these tensions to surface and to be expressed. In more authoritarian classrooms, students may simply reject what is offered as knowledge and not engage in dialogue. And though these feminist teachers do not always recognize the intended meanings or readings of their students on issues of class and race, they constantly struggle to address these issues and to make their classrooms, in the words of one of the teachers, places where "it's okay to be human."

I think it is important to recognize the fundamental philosophy of teaching that emerges from this kind of recognition of multiple oppressions. While these teachers and administrators encourage a rigorous critique and analysis of texts that can stand up to the standards of conventional views of academic analysis, they do not envision teaching as solely the transmission of "facts," or of the knowledge of the dominant culture of the United States—white, male, Euro-centered, middle class. The basis of their work is a recognition of the value of students' own voices, subjective experiences of power and oppression, and the worth of their class and ethnic cultures. We can see in the practice of these teachers and administrators the outline of teaching as transformative work in which what is most significant is the building of the capacity for critique and self-critique. Thus, like Freire, these teachers seek a dialogue with students and encourage them to unravel and understand the dynamics of their own life histories. Equally important in making possible this critical pedagogy is the work of women administrators who support classroom teachers, introduce new materials, and create an atmosphere in which progressive teaching is encouraged. The work of these administrators points to the importance of creating a community within schools in which progressive teachers and administrators who share common goals can find support and can see that their work is valued and rewarded.

The qualities that have been associated with feminist pedagogy are central to the kind of transformative teaching these teachers and administrators hope to accomplish. This teaching reflects feminist values in pedagogy as well as content. Their work recalls Schniedewind's description of feminist teaching: "Feminism is taught through process as well as formal content. To reflect feminist values in teaching is to teach progressively, democratically, and with feeling." (Schniedewind, 1983, p. 271) In their work, these feminist teachers raise issues of sexism and racism directly in texts, but also in classroom relationships and in their willingness to share their own beliefs and experiences with students. As feminists they make the gendered subjectivities of themselves and their students part of the texts they teach. And at the same time, they ground a critical inquiry in a deep respect for their students' lives and cultural values.

In the work of these feminist teachers and in the conflicts that arise in their classrooms, the outline of a critical pedagogy emerges. This critical pedagogy rests on a recognition of the multiple subjectivities of students and teachers. It makes as part of its text the inherent tensions of U.S. society that are expressed in classroom discourse in the public schools. As teachers seek to develop this critical pedagogy, they recognize students' multiple subjectivies and the ways in which different forms of oppression may come into conflict in classrooms. Their teaching calls to mind the critical pedagogy called for by Giroux and Aronowitz:

> A critical pedagogy . . . would focus on the study of curriculum not merely as a matter of self-cultivation or the mimicry of specific forms of language and knowledge. On the contrary, it would stress forms of learning and knowledge aimed at providing a critical understanding of how social reality works, it would focus on how certain dimensions of such a reality are sustained, it would focus on the nature of its formative processes, and it would also focus on how those aspects of it that are related to the logic of domination can be changed. (Aronowitz and Giroux, 1985, p. 217)

Setting individuals and groups against one another according to their gender or race has marked U.S. society from the beginning. In these schools, we see those conflicts replicated as white women or girls oppressed by sexism are separated from and set against black men and boys oppressed by racism. And black women must struggle against both racism and sexism. The same individuals can be empowered in part of their subjectivity while oppressed by another part. The complexity of these lived subjectivies in an unequal and oppressive society must be recognized for critical pedagogy to be developed. Teachers and administrators attempting to develop a critical pedagogy need to emphasize that the conflicts expressed in democratic and critical classrooms emerge from the exploitative and oppressive quality of U.S. society in general. These conflicts reflect real forms of oppression and inequality, and a classroom which encourages the exploration of each student's own subjectivity will draw out these contradictions and tensions. Thus a critical pedagogy needs to make these conflicts themselves part of the text of critical teaching.

The historical development and political function of the public schools in U.S. society as state institutions has been well documented through both historical and theoretical studies. (Tyack, 1974; Nassaw, 1979; Callahan, 1962; Feinberg, 1975; Kliebard, 1971; Katz, 1968, 1971; Bowles and Gintis, 1976) As state institutions, they reflect the logic of state power within a certain economic formation, in this case, capitalism. Their hierarchical structure, the content of the formal curriculum, the nature of the hidden curriculum of rules and social relationships all tend to reproduce the status quo. In this society, that entails the reproduction of existing class, racial, and gender divisions. Those who are in control, who dominate and benefit from this structure, attempt in both conscious and unconscious ways to shape the schools so as to maintain their own privilege. In this way, school organization and practices tend to reproduce and justify classism, racism, and sexism, those features which so characterize contemporary U.S. society.

The difficulties of teaching in this present climate have been enumerated in a number of recent studies. (Apple, 1982; Aronowitz and Giroux, 1985; Freedman, 1985; Cohen, 1985) Increasing administrative control over curriculum, the movement toward quantifiable results and the use of standardized testing all must be struggled against. These forms of de-skilling undercut the possibilities of the classroom by taking control of knowledge out of the hands of teachers. They dehumanize both students and teachers and challenge the very possibility of critical pedagogy. High school teachers in general face constraints and pressures that are well documented and are increasing. These constraints create a teaching situation that is markedly different from that faced by college and university teachers. Most obvious of these differences are the much more powerful structures of curricular, administrative, and parental control in high school classrooms. High school teachers are not considered scholars or independent authorities—quite the contrary; increasingly they are seen as functionaries in a technocratic vision of schooling in which they have to meet certain prescribed goals (are the test results of their students rising?); and women teachers are all too often seen as a traditional nurturing presence under the "expert guidance" of male administrators and academics. But their valuable work as intellectuals attempting to encourage critical analysis of texts and society is rarely recognized. Progressive high school administrators must struggle with public expectations and criticisms of schools as the institutions supposedly responsible for a variety of social and economic problems. Thus feminist teachers and administrators, like all progressive workers in schools, too often work without public understanding or recognition of their work and find themselves in opposition to an increasingly narrow definition of schooling as the means of reproducing a trained work force for U.S. capitalism.

However, the deep irony of the schools is that while they are state institutions in many respects intended for social reproduction and control, they are also at the same time sites where education can occur. Both teachers and students are human beings who create meaning and who can reshape the knowledge and values of the past for their own uses. By their very definition, schools encourage literacy and make available texts and knowledge. While this knowledge may be imposed in forms that Freire has called domestication, it is not inevitable that this be the case. As we have seen in the work of these feminist teachers, the classroom can become a site for the interrogation of texts, and for the encouragement of critique as students and teachers struggle to create their own meaning and understand their own history and culture. In all these ways schools can be public sites for the creation of what Aronowitz and Giroux call "the discourse of possibility." Learning and teaching *can* take place in the interests of human liberation, even within institutions created for social control. What this study illustrates is the complexity of that project and the need to recognize and to fight for critical teaching and learning as a means of empowerment.

The empowerment of students means encouraging them to explore and analyze the forces acting upon their lives. It means respecting and legitimizing students' own voices in the classroom. But the empowerment of students also must entail the empowerment of teachers. Teachers need to have their work as intellectuals respected and recognized. Teaching is valuable and highly political work and both teachers and those outside the schools need to recognize the value of that work. But teaching as political work entails more than simply what goes on in isolated classrooms (what Steedman once refered to as her little "socialist republic." [1985]) Classroom teachers need to break out of the isolation of their own classrooms. As Freedman, Jackson and Boles have documented so well, traditionally teaching has been organized to encourage isolation and competition among teachers. For their own empowerment and in order to organize against the increasing bureaucratization of schools, progressive teachers and administrators must seek out ways of working collectively and collaboratively. This is true both in terms of curriculum and the social relationships of the classroom, but also in terms of the hierarchical structures of the schools themselves. If teachers and administrators call for critique and democratic relationships from their students, they must also struggle for those things with their own colleagues. And this, of course, also means struggling with the existing oppressions of the school itself, the sexism and racism among teachers and administrators which are expressed both in institutional structure and in daily practices. The experiences of these women teachers and administrators highlights these tensions, as they experience sexism (and, in the case of women of color, racism as well) both in their life histories and in their present work. Bringing these forms of oppression to light will create the same kinds of tensions that will arise in critical, democratic classrooms. But unless they are addressed, they cannot really be effectively struggled against or changed.

One of the major intentions of this study was to document the work of feminist teachers and administrators and to uncover the nature of women's experiences in patriarchal institutions. In this sense, this work is part of the feminist project described in chapter three, to make women the focus of study, not as the "other" in an androcentric world, but as subjects and the center of this social reality. In Adrienne Rich's words, women need "concrete artifacts, the work of hands, written words to read, images to look at, a dialogue with brave and imaginative women who came before us." (Rich, 1979, p. 205) In this respect, this study is meant to move beyond feminist studies which view schools as simply the site of the reproduction of gender oppression or which celebrate the resistance of girls to schools as oppressive patriarchal institutions intended to reproduce both class and gender oppression. Instead, by focusing on the lives and work of feminist teachers and administrators, I want to reveal them as "brave and imaginative women" and to point to the ways in which a feminist counter-hegemony is being struggled for in the public schools. As we saw, this is not achieved unproblematically; both the institutional structure of the school and the competing subjectivities of the students themselves make feminist teaching a challenge in the public schools. But the work of these humane and sympathetic teachers and administrators should be acknowledged, both as a tribute to their own struggle and achievements and as a reminder that human beings reflect, critique, and to whatever limited extent, make their own history.

The conclusions of this study will, I hope, be useful to other feminist and progressive teachers. For me, one of the insights of this work came from observing graphically the ways in which the classrooms of public high schools concentrate the tensions and contradictions of U.S. society as a whole. The lived oppression and power of students and teachers were constantly manifested in classroom discourse. The forces that shape our lives were evident in this discourse, in the institutional structure of schools, and in the life histories of teachers. A society so shaped by racism, sexism, classism, and with great economic, political, and military power in the hands of a few cannot be transformed by the most dedicated and critical teaching alone. I think it is vital that feminist and other progressive teachers remember the power that social forces exert on themselves and on their students and that they recognize the limits of what it is possible to accomplish in a classroom. But by recognizing the limits of what is possible, teachers (and all of us) should recognize the value and importance of *doing* what is possible. In this way, I would like this study to document not only the richness and significance of these women's lives and work, but to provide examples of the need and possibility of struggling against forces of oppression in all spheres.

# Bibliography

Acker, Sandra. No-woman's land: British sociology of education 1960–1979. *The Sociological Review* (1981) 29, 1.

———. Women and education. In Anthony Hartnett, ed. *The social sciences in educational studies*. London: Heinemann Educational Books, 1982.

———. Women and teaching: A semi-detached sociology of a semi-profession. In Stephen Walker and Len Barton, eds. *Gender class and education*. Lewes, Sussex: Falmer Press, 1983.

Adamson, Walter. *Hegemony and revolution*. Berkeley: Univ. of California Press, 1980.

Althusser, Louis. Ideology and ideological state apparatuses. In Louis Althusser. *Lenin and philosophy and other essays*. New York: Monthly Review Press, 1971.

Amos, Valerie and Parmar, Pratibha. Resistances and responses: The experiences of black girls in Britain. In Angela McRobbie and Trisha McCabe, eds., *Feminism for girls*. London and Boston: Routledge and Kegan Paul, 1981.

Anderson, Perry. *Arguments within English Marxism*. London: Verso Press, 1980.

Annas, Pam. Style as politics: A feminist approach to the teaching of writing. *College English* (1985) 47, 4, 360–371.

Anyon, Jean. Intersections of gender and class: Accommodation and resistance by working class and affluent females to contradictory sex-role ideologies. *Journal of Education* (1984) 166, 1, 25–48.

Apple, Michael. *Ideology and curriculum*. London and Boston: Routledge and Kegan Paul, 1979.

———. Curricular form and the logic of technical control: Building the possessive individual. In Michael Apple, ed. *Cultural and economic reproduction in education*. London and Boston: Routledge and Kegan Paul, 1982.

———. *Education and power*. London and Boston: Routledge and Kegan Paul, 1982.

Arnot, Madeleine. See also MacDonald

———. Male hegemony, social class and women's education. *Journal of Education* (1982) 164, 1, 64–89.

———. Feminist perspectives and the political economy of women's education. *Journal of Education* (1984) 166, 1, 5–25.

Aronowitz, Stanley and Giroux, Henry. *Education under siege: The conservative, liberal and radical debate over schooling*. South Hadley, Mass.: Bergin and Garvey, 1985.

Bakhtin, Mikhail. *The dialogic imagination*. Austin: Univ. of Texas Press, 1981.

Barrett, Michele. *Women's oppression today*. London: Virago Press, 1980.

Barthes, Roland. *Mythologies*. London: Paladin Books, 1973.

Belotti, Elena. *Little girls*. London: Readers and Writers Publishing Cooperative, 1975.

Bates, Richard. New developments in the new sociology of education. *British Journal of Sociology of Education* (1980) 1, 1.

Bennett, Adrian and Sola, Michele. The struggle for voice: Narrative, literacy and consciousness in an East Harlem school. *Journal of Education* (1985) 167, 1, 88–110.

Bernstein, Basil. *Class, codes and control. vol. 3*. London and Boston: Routledge and Kegan Paul, 1979.

Bisseret, Noelle. *Education, class language and ideology*. London and Boston: Routledge and Kegan Paul, 1979.

Black, Maria and Coward, Rosalind. Linguistic, social and sexual relations: A review of Dale Spender's *Man made language*. *Screen Education* (1981) 39, 69–81.

Boggs, Carl. *Gramsci's marxism*. London: Pluto Press, 1976.

Bourdieu, Pierre and Passeron, Jean-Claude. *Reproduction in education society and culture*. London and Beverly Hills: Sage Publications, 1977.

Bowles, Gloria and Dueli-Klein, Renate. *Theories of women's studies*. London and Boston: Routledge and Kegan Paul, 1983.

Bowles, Samuel and Gintis, Herbert. *Schooling in capitalist America*. New York: Basic Books, 1976.

Brah, Avtar and Minhas, Rehana. Structural racism or cultural difference: Schooling for Asian girls. In Gaby Weiner, ed. *Just a bunch of girls*. Milton Keynes: Open University Press, 1985.

Brake, Mike. *The sociology of youth culture and youth subcultures*. London and Boston: Routledge and Kegan Paul, 1980.

Brooks, Betty and Sievers, Sharon. The new right challenges women's studies: The Long Beach women's studies program. In Charlotte Bunch, and Sandra Pollack, eds. *Learning our way*. Trumansburg, N.Y.: Crossing Press, 1983.

Bunch, Charlotte. Not by degrees: Feminist theory and education. In Charlotte Bunch and Sandra Pollack, eds. *Learning our way*. Trumansburg, N. Y.: Crossing Press, 1983.

Bunch, Charlotte and Pollack, Sandra, eds. *Learning our way*. Trumansburg, N.Y.: Crossing Press, 1983.

Byrne, Eileen. *Women and education*. London: Tavistock, 1978

Callahan, Raymond. *Education and the cult of efficiency.* Chicago: Univ. of Chicago Press, 1962.

Chetwynd, Jane and Harnett, Oonagh. *The sex role system.* London and Boston: Routledge and Kegan Paul, 1978.

Chodorow, Nancy. *The reproduction of mothering.* Berkeley: Univ. of California Press, 1978.

Clark, John, Crichter, Chas, and Johnson, Richard. *Working class culture.* London: Hutchison, 1979.

Cloward, Richard and Piven, Frances Fox. Hidden protest: The channeling of female innovation and resistance. *Signs* (1979) 4, 4, 651–669.

Cohen, David. Greater expectations. *The Nation* (25 May 1985) 240, 20, 615–622.

Connell, R. W. *Teachers' work.* London: George Allen and Unwin, 1985.

Connell, R. W., Dowsett, G. W., Kessler, S., and Aschenden, D. J. *Making the difference.* Boston: Allen and Unwin, 1982.

David, Miriam. *The state, the family and education.* London: Routledge and Kegan Paul, 1980.

Davies, Lynn. Gender, resistance and power. In Stephen Walker and Len Barton, eds. *Gender class and education.* Lewes, Sussex: The Falmer Press, 1983.

DeBeauvoir, Simone. *The second sex.* New York: Bantam Books, 1961.

Deem, Rosemary. Introduction. *Schooling for women's work.* London and Boston: Routledge and Kegan Paul, 1980.

———. *Women and schooling.* London and Boston: Routledge and Kegan Paul, 1978.

Delamont, Sara. *Sex roles and the school.* London: Methuen, 1980.

Dinnerstein, Dorothy. *The mermaid and the minotaur.* New York: Harper Colophon Books, 1976.

Dreeben, Robert. *On what is learned in school.* Reading, Mass: Addison and Wesley, 1968.

DuBois, Barbara. Passionate scholarship: Notes on values, knowing and method in feminist social science. In Gloria Bowles and Renate Dueli-Klein, eds. *Theories of women's studies.* London and Boston: Routledge and Kegan Paul, 1983.

Dueli-Klein, Renate. How to do what we want to do: Thoughts about feminist methodology. In Gloria Bowles and Renate Dueli-Klein, eds. *Theories of women's studies.* London and Boston: Routledge and Kegan Paul, 1979.

Ehrenreich, Barbara. Life without father: Reconsidering socialist-feminist theory. *Socialist Review* (Jan.–Feb., 1984) 73, 48–58.

Eisenstein, Zillah. ed. *Capitalist patriarchy and the case for socialist feminism.* New York and London: Monthly Review Press, 1979.

Esland, Geoff. Teaching and learning as the organization of knowledge. In Michael Young, ed. *Knowledge and control.* London: Collier Macmillan, 1971.

Evans, Sara. *Personal politics.* New York: Vintage Books, 1980.

Everhart, Robert. *Reading, writing and resistance.* London and Boston: Routledge and Kegan Paul, 1983.

Feinberg, Walter. *Reason and rhetoric.* New York: Wiley and Son, 1975.

Foster, Marina. A curriculum for all? The relationship between racism, feminism and schooling: A personal view. In Gaby Weiner, ed. *Just a bunch of girls.* Milton Keynes: The Open University Press, 1985.

Frankenstein, Marilyn. Critical mathematics eduction: An application of Paulo Freire's epistemology. *Journal of Education* (1983) 165, 4, 315–340.

Frazier, Nancy and Sadker, Myra. *Sexism in school and society.* New York: Harper and Row, 1973.

Freedman, Sara. Master teacher/merit pay—weeding out women from "women's 'true' profession." *Radical Teacher,* 25 (1985), 24–29.

Freedman, Sara, Jackson, Jane, and Boles, Catherine. *The effects of the institutional structure of schools on teachers.* Boston: Boston Women's Teachers Group, 1982.

Freire, Paulo. *Pedagogy of the oppressed.* New York: Harper and Row, 1971.

———. *Education for critical consciousness.* New York: Seabury Press, 1973.

———. *Pedagogy in process: The letters from Guinea-Bissau.* New York: Seabury Press, 1978.

———. The importance of the act of reading. *Journal of Education* (1983) 165, 1, 5–11.

———. *The politics of education.* South Hadley, Mass.: Bergin and Garvey, 1985.

Fuller, Mary. Black girls in a London comprehensive school. In Rosemary Deem, ed. *Schooling for women's work.* London and Boston: Routledge and Kegan Paul, 1980.

———. Qualified criticism, critical qualifications. In Jane Purvis and Margaret Hales. *Achievement and inequality in education.* London: Routledge and Kegan Paul, 1983.

Gaskell, Jane. Course enrollment in the high school: The perspective of working class females. *Sociology of Education* (1985) 58, 1, 48–59.

Gates, Barbara, Klaw, Susan, and Steinberg, Adria. *Changing learning, changing lives.* Old Westbury, N.Y.: Feminist Press, 1979.

Giddens, Anthony. *Central problems in social theory.* Berkeley: Univ. of California Press, 1979.

Gilligan, Carol. *In a different voice.* Cambridge: Harvard Univ. Press, 1980.

Gilmore, Perry. Spelling "Mississippi": Recontextualizing a literacy-related speech event. *Anthropology and Education Quarterly,* (1983) 14, 235–255.

Giroux, Henry. *Ideology, culture and the process of schooling.* Philadelphia: Temple Univ. Press, 1981.

———. Ideology and agency in the process of schooling. *Journal of Education* (1982) 165, 1, 12–35.

———. *Theory, resistance, and education.* South Hadley, Mass.: Bergin and Garvey, 1983.

———. Marxism and schooling: The limits of radical educational discourse. *Educational Theory* (1985) 34, 2, 113–135.

Gitlin, Todd. Prime-time ideology: The hegemonic process in television entertainment. *Social Problems* (1979) 26–49.

Gramsci, Antonio. *Selections from the prison notebooks.* Quintin Hoare and Geoff Nowell-Smith, eds. New York: International Publishers, 1971.

————. *Selections from cultural writings.* David Forgacs and Geoff Nowell-Smith, eds. Cambridge, Mass.: Harvard Univ. Press, 1985.

Gornick, Vivian. Women as outsiders. In Vivian Gornick and Barbara Moran, eds. *Women in sexist society.* New York: Basic Books, 1971.

Hall, Stuart and Jefferson, Tony. *Resistance through ritual.* London: Hutchison, 1976.

Hall, Stuart, Hobson, Dorothy, Lowe, Andrew, and Willis, Paul. *Culture, media, language.* London: Hutchison, 1980.

Hartsock, Nancy. Feminist theory and the development of revolutionary strategy. In Zillah Eisenstein, ed. *Capitalist patriarchy and the case for socialist feminism.* London and New York: Monthly Review Press, 1979.

————. *Money, sex and power.* Boston: Northeastern Univ. Press, 1983.

Hartmann, Heidi. The unhappy marriage of socialism and feminism. In Lydia Sargent, ed. *Women and Revolution.* Boston: South End Press, 1981.

Hebdidge, Dick. *Subcultures.* London and New York: Methuen, 1979.

Hochschild, Arlie. The sociology of feeling and emotion: Selected possibilities. In Marcia Millman and Rosabeth Kanter, eds. *Another voice: Feminist perspectives on social life and social science.* New York: Anchor Books, 1975.

hooks, bell. *Feminist theory from margin to center.* Boston: South End Press, 1984.

Hull, Gloria, Scott, Patricia, and Smith, Barbara. *All the women are white, all the blacks are men, but some of us are brave.* New York: The Feminist Press, 1982.

Jagger, Alison. *Feminist theory and human nature.* Sussex: Harvester Press, 1983.

Johnson, Richard. What is cultural studies anyway? *Anglistica,* XXVI, 1–2 (1983).

————. Really useful knowledge: Radical education and working class culture 1790–1848. In John Clark, Chas Crichter, and Richard Johnson, eds. *Working class culture.* London: Hutchison, 1979.

Jordan, June. *Civil wars.* Boston: The Beacon Press, 1981.

Katz, Michael. *The irony of early school reform.* Cambridge: Harvard Univ. Press, 1968.

————. *Class, bureaucracy and the schools.* New York: Praeger, 1971.

Keddie, Nell. Classroom knowledge. In Michael Young, ed. *Knowledge and control.* London: Collier Macmillan, 1971.

Kelly, Gayle and Nihlen, Ann. Schooling and the reproduction of patriarchy: Unequal workloads, unequal rewards. In Michael Apple, ed. *Cultural and economic reproduction in education.* London and Boston: Routledge and Kegan Paul, 1982.

Kessler, S., Ashenden, R., Connell, R., and Dowsett, G. Gender relations in secondary schooling. *Sociology of Education* (1985) 58, 1, 34–48.

Kliebard, Herbert. Bureaucracy and curriculum theory. In Vernon Hautrick, ed. *Freedom, bureaucracy, and schooling.* Washington: Association for Supervision and Curriculum Development, 1971.

Komarovsky, Mirra. *Blue collar marriage.* New York: Vintage Press, 1967.

Kuhn, Annette and Wolpe, AnnMarie, eds. *Feminism and materialism*. London and Boston: Routledge and Kegan Paul, 1978.

Lather, Patti. Critical theory, curricular transformation and feminist mainstreaming. *Journal of Education* (1984) 166, 1, 49–62.

Levy, Betty. The school's role in the sex-role stereotyping of girls: A feminist review of the literature. *Feminist Studies* (1972) 1, 5–23.

Mahony, Pat. *Schools for the boys? Coeducation reassessed*. London: Hutchison, 1985.

Mannicom, Ann. Feminist frameworks and teacher education. *Journal of Education* (1984) 166, 1, 77–89.

MacDonald, Madeleine. (Later Arnot) Cultural reproduction: The pedagogy of sexuality. *Screen Education* (1979/80) 17–30.

———. Socio-cultural reproduction and women's education. In Rosemary Deem, ed. *Schooling for women's work*. Boston and London: Routledge and Kegan Paul, 1980.

———. Schooling and the reproduction of class and gender relations. In Madeleine MacDonald, Roger Dale, Geoff Esland, and Ross Fergusson, eds. *Politics, patriarchy, and practice*. Lewes, Sussex: Falmer Press, 1981.

McRobbie, Angela. Working class girls and the culture of femininity. In Centre for Contemporary Cultural Studies Women's Group. *Women take issue*. London: Hutchison, 1978.

———. Settling accounts with subcultures. *Screen Education* (1980) 34, 37–51.

———. Just like a *Jackie* story. In Angela McRobbie and Trisha McCabe, eds. *Feminism for girls*. London and Boston: Routledge and Kegan Paul, 1981.

McRobbie, Angela and Garber, Jenny. Girls and subcultures. In Stuart Hall and Tony Jefferson, eds. *Resistance through rituals*. London: Hutchison, 1975.

Marx, Karl. The eighteenth Brumaire of Louis Bonaparte. In Robert Tucker, ed. *The Marx-Engels reader*. New York: Norton and Company, 1972.

Mies, Maria. Toward a methodology for feminist research. In Gloria Bowles and Renate Dueli-Klein, eds. *Theories of women's studies*. London and Boston: Routledge and Kegan Paul, 1983.

Millet, Kate. *Sexual politics*. New York: Avon Books, 1970.

Moraga, Cherrie and Anzaldua, Gloria, eds. *This bridge called my back: Writings by radical women of color*. Watertown, Mass.: Persephone Press, 1981.

Mouffe, Chantal. *Gramsci and Marxist theory*. London and Boston: Routledge and Kegan Paul, 1979.

Nassaw, David. *Schooled to order*. Oxford and New York: Oxford Univ. Press, 1979.

The National Commission on Excellence in Education. *A nation at risk*. Washington, D.C.: United States Department of Education, 1983.

Oakley, Ann. Interviewing women: A contradiction in terms. In Helen Roberts, ed. *Doing feminist research*. London and Boston: Routledge and Kegan Paul, 1981.

O' Brien, Mary. *The politics of reproduction*. London and Boston: Routledge and Kegan Paul, 1983.

Pollack, Sandra. Exposing the conservative agenda: Women's studies minus feminism. *Radical Teacher* (1985) 29, 19–24.

Popkewitz, Thomas. Educational reform as the organization of ritual: Stability as change. *Journal of Education* (1982) 164, 1, 5–30.

Reiter, Rayna, ed. *Toward an anthropology of women.* New York and London: Monthly Review Press, 1975.

Rich, Adrienne. *On lies, secrets, and silence.* New York: Norton, 1979.

Riley, Kathryn. Black girls speak for themselves. In Gaby Weiner, ed. *Just a bunch of girls.* Milton Keynes: Open University Press, 1985.

Rofel, Lisa and Weston, Kathleen. Sexuality, class and conflict in a lesbian workplace. *Signs* (1984) 9, 4, 623–646.

Rowbotham, Sheila. *Women's consciousness, man's world.* London: Penguin Books, 1973.

Rowbotham, Sheila, Segal, Lynne, and Wainwright, Hilary. *Beyond the fragments: Feminism and the making of socialism.* Boston: Alyson Publications, 1981.

Rubin, Gayle. The traffic in women: Notes on the political economy of sex. In Rayna Reiter, ed. *Toward an anthropology of women.* New York and London: Monthly Review Press, 1975.

Rubin, Lilian. *Worlds of pain.* New York: Basic Books, 1976.

Russell, Michelle. Black-eyed blues connection: From the inside out. In Charlotte Bunch and Sandra Pollack, eds. *Learning our way: Essays in feminist education.* Trumansburg, N.Y.: Crossing Press, 1983.

Schniedewind, Nancy. Feminist values: Guidelines for teaching methodology in women's studies. In Charlotte Bunch and Sandra Pollack, eds. *Learning our way: Essays in feminist education.* Trumansburg, N.Y.: Crossing Press, 1983.

Schniedewind, Nancy. and Davidson, Ellen. *Open minds to equality: Learning activities to promote race, sex, class and age equality.* Englewood Cliffs, N.J.: Prentice Hall, 1983.

Sennett, Richard and Cobb, Jonathan. *The hidden injuries of class.* 1973; reprint ed., Madison: Univ. of Wisconsin Press, 1979.

Shor, Ira. *Critical teaching and everyday life.* Boston: South End Press, 1980.

Simon, Roger. But who will let you do it? Counter-hegemonic possibilities for work education. *Journal of Education* (1983) 165, 3, 235–256.

Smith, Dorothy. A sociology for women. In Julia Sherman and Evelyn Beck, eds. *The prism of sex: Essays in the sociology of knowledge.* Madison: Univ. of Wisconsin Press, 1977.

———. The everyday world as problematic: A feminist method. Paper read at Boston Area Colloquium on Feminist Theory, 13 February 1986. Northeastern University, Boston, Mass.

Spanier, Bonnie, Bloom, Alex, and Boroviak, Darlene. *Toward a balanced curriculum.* Cambridge, Mass.: Schenkman Publishing Company, 1984.

Spender, Dale and Sarah, Elizabeth, eds. *Learning to lose.* London: The Womens Press, 1980.

Stanley, Liz and Wise, Sue. *Breaking out: Feminist consciousness and feminist research.* London and Boston: Routledge and Kegan Paul, 1983.

Steedman, Carolyn. Prisonhouses. *Feminist Review* (1985) 20, 7–21.

Strober, Myra and Tyack, David. Why do women teach and men manage? *Signs* (1980) 5, 3, 494–503.

Tanner, David and Tanner, Laurel. *Curriculum development.* New York: Macmillan, 1980.

Task Force on Education for Economic Growth. *Action for excellence; A comprehensive plan to improve our nation's schools.* Denver: Education Commission of the States, 1983.

Tax, Meredith. Learning how to bake. *Socialist Review* (Jan.-Feb. 1984) 73, 36–41.

Thompson, Edward. *The poverty of theory.* London: Merlin Press, 1978.

Thomas, Claire. Girls and counter-school culture. *Melbourne Working Papers.* Melbourne, 1980.

Tyack, David. *The one best system.* Cambridge: Harvard Univ. Press, 1974.

Tyler, Ralph. *Basic principles of curriculum and instruction.* Chicago: Univ. of Chicago Press, 1950.

Walkerdine, Valerie. Sex, power and pedagogy. *Screen Education* (Spring, 1981) 38–51.

Walker, Alice. *In search of our mother's gardens.* New York: Harcourt, Brace, Jovanovich, 1983.

Walker, Stephen and Barton, Len. *Gender class and education.* Lewes, Sussex: Falmer Press, 1983.

Weiner, Gaby. ed. *Just a bunch of girls: Feminist approaches to schooling.* Milton Keynes: Open University Press, 1985.

Wescott, Marcia. Feminist criticism of the social sciences. *Harvard Educational Review* (1979) 49, 4, 422–430.

Wexler, Philip and Whitson, Tony. Hegemony and education. *Psychology and Social Theory,* 1982, 3, 31–42.

Whitty, Geoff. Sociology and the problem of radical educational change. In Michael Young and Geoff Whitty, eds. *Society, state and schooling.* Lewes, Sussex: Falmer Press, 1977.

Whyte, Judith, Deem, Rosemary, Kant, Lesley, Cruickshank, Maureen, eds. *Girl friendly schooling.* London: Methuen, 1985.

Williams, Raymond. *Marxism and literature.* Oxford: Oxford Univ. Press, 1977.

Willis, Paul. *Learning to labour.* Westmead, England: Saxon House, 1977.

———. Cultural production is different from cultural reproduction is different from social reproduction is different from production. *Interchange* (1981) 12, 2–3, 48–68.

Wilson, Deirdre. Sexual codes and conduct: A study of teenage girls. In Carol Smart and Barry Smart, eds. *Women, sexuality and social control.* London and Boston: Routledge and Kegan Paul, 1978.

Wolpe, AnnMarie. The official ideology of education for girls. In Madeleine McDonald, Roger Dale, Geoff Esland, and Ross Fergusson, eds. *Politics, patriarchy and practice.* Lewes, Sussex: The Falmer Press, 1981.

———. Education and the sexual division of labour. In Annette Kuhn and AnnMarie Wolpe, eds. *Feminism and materialism.* Boston and London: Routledge and Kegan Paul, 1978.

Wolpe, AnnMarie and Kuhn, Annette. Feminism and materialism. In Annette

Kuhn and AnnMarie Wolpe, eds. *Feminism and materialism.* Boston and London: Routledge and Kegan Paul, 1978.
Women's Study Group. *Women take issue.* London: CCCS/Hutchison, 1978.
Young, Michael. ed. *Knowledge and control.* London: Collier Macmillan, 1971.

# Index

Accommodation: Anyon on, 49–50; Fuller on, 47

Adamson, Walter, 13

Althusser, Louis, 5, 6–8, 20, 22; on consciousness and social circumstances, 74; criticisms of, 8; functionalism in, 8; on ideological state apparatuses, 7; influence on Barrett, 32; influence on Wolpe, 34; on reproduction of class relationships, 7; on role of schools, 6; theory of ideology, 7; use of concept of problematique, 30

Amos, Valerie, and Parmar, Pratibha, 48

Anyon, Jean, 48–49

Apple Michael, 21; on hegemony, 17

Arnot, Madeleine, 28, 32, 38–39; on class analysis, 64; on concept of male hegemony, 125; critique of social reproduction theories, 38; influence of Bernstein on, 38; influence of Bourdieu on, 38

Bakhtin, Mikhail, 129; on intentions of discourse, 139

Banking education, 127

Barrett, Michele, 32; influence of Althusser on, 32

Bates, Richard, 12

Bennett, Adrian, and Sola, Michele, 129

# Other Books of Interest from Bergin & Garvey

**WOMEN'S WORK**
ELEANOR LEACOCK, HELEN I. SAFA
& CONTRIBUTORS
*320 pages      Photographs*

**ACADEMIC WOMEN:**
**Working Towards Equality**
ANGELA SIMEONE
*176 pages*

**WOMEN & CHANGE IN LATIN**
**AMERICA**
JUNE NASH, HELEN I. SAFA
& CONTRIBUTORS
*384 pages      Photographs*

**WOMEN & MEN AS LEADERS**
TRUDY HELLER
*224 pages*

**CAREER PATTERNS IN**
**EDUCATION**
FLORA IDA ORTIZ
*196 pages*

**WOMEN & COLONIZATION**
MONA ETIENNE, ELEANOR LEACOCK
& CONTRIBUTORS
*352 pages      Illustrations*

**BOYS & GIRLS AT PLAY**
EVELYN GOODENOUGH PITCHER
& LYNN HICKEY SCHULTZ
*224 pages*

**UNEQUAL ACCESS:**
**Women Lawyers in a Changing**
**America**
RONALD CHESTER
*160 pages*